"Want expert advice on how to live to 100? You're in luck! Here's an appointment with Dr. Jerry Kornfeld, an experienced practicing physician and university professor, who is internationally recognized as a skilled communicator of medical wisdom. Your 100-Year Heart explains in easy-to-follow steps how you can avoid or even reverse damage to your heart-- it's a century's worth of invaluable counsel!

James B. Maas, PhD
Weiss Presidential Fellow
Professor and past-chair of Psychology
Cornell University

"This book could save your life, if you're willing to help yourself."

Michael J. Soltero M.D.
Director Cardiovascular Surgery
Northridge Hospital Medical Center

Dennis

A Toast to
your 100th Birthday

Jerry Lyfel

YOUR 100-YEAR HEART

SIMPLE steps for keeping your heart ALIVE and WELL,
based on 35 years of EXPERIENCES as a practicing
physician

by

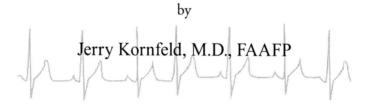

Jerry Kornfeld, M.D., FAAFP

Bloomington, IN   Milton Keynes, UK

authorHOUSE®

AuthorHouse™
1663 Liberty Drive, Suite 200
Bloomington, IN 47403
www.authorhouse.com
Phone: 1-800-839-8640

AuthorHouse™ UK Ltd.
500 Avebury Boulevard
Central Milton Keynes, MK9 2BE
www.authorhouse.co.uk
Phone: 08001974150

First published by AuthorHouse 11/20/2006

ISBN: 978-1-4259-5649-3 (sc)

Library of Congress Control Number: 2006908747

*Printed in the United States of America
Bloomington, Indiana*

This book is printed on acid-free paper.

DEDICATION

To my lifelong companion and love, my wife Millie and to my 2 daughters, Judy and Linda, whose love has been the inspiration for a joyous life, I dedicate this book.

ACKNOWLEDGMENTS

I am continually amazed how exciting life can be, if only one allows it to happen.

I had spent the past 30 years as a family physician in the trenches of clinical medicine. One evening I was approached by good friends, Susan and Gary Reuben. They were active in Vistage (AKA TEC International), a worldwide organization of CEOs and were curious, based on my experiences as an educator in the academic and TV worlds, if I would be interested in speaking to one of these groups. After they explained what Vistage was all about, and that it was the premier organizations of CEOs in the world, I was very excited to appear before them.

That was the beginning of a very exciting speaking career. The chair of the first group I spoke to was Bill Hall, a dynamic leader. The response I received from him and his group was overwhelming. I found them, and subsequent groups, to be unique. Never before had I experienced an audience with such intensity. They accepted nothing at face value and asked deep, penetrating questions.

Six years have passed and I have given over 250 talks to Vistage groups around the world. My speaking career has taken me down a very exciting path. I now have frequent requests to appear before numerous other groups both on land and on sea. Yes, life is exciting!

Based upon the countless comments and requests for medical information that I have received from all of these organizations, I would be remiss if I did not acknowledge the part they have played in my writing this book. Their encouragement, intellectual stimulation and response to my message have played a very important role in my finally sitting down and completing this project. To all of you out there let me say; Thank you for allowing me to touch your lives

In addition, thank you to my editor Cliff Carle, Elaine Freund, Dr. Len Skaist, and to a dear, departed friend, comedy writer Milt Rosen. Milt was the co-author of my first book The Fatherhood Formula. His wit, intellect and sense of caring were admired by all who had the good fortune to know him

And finally, to my life long partner, my wife Millie. For putting up with me and my constant request to listen, read and advise on each chapter. For her artistic skills in designing the front cover, for her patience with my frequent episodes of frustration, when things were not going well, and for all of her other acts of kindness, I humbly say THANK YOU

Contents

INTRODUCTION

So who is Dr. Jerry Kornfeld, and why is he writing this book?

First my credentials. I am a graduate of the School of Public Health at UCLA with a Bachelor of Science degree, and the School of Medicine at UCI with an M.D. degree. I did my postgraduate training at Los Angeles County General Hospital. It was there I realized that the study of the heart and how it functions to keep us alive was going to be the area of my greatest interest. I have spent the past 35 years practicing as a board-certified family physician in the suburbs of Los Angeles. Currently, I am a faculty member of the UCLA School of Medicine. In addition to being a clinician and educator, I have been an author and a television commentator on medical issues. I have spent the last five years traveling around the world speaking to corporate and general audiences about their most important asset: their heart.

Now that you know a little about my academic background, let me share with you my fascination with the heart. First and foremost, the heart is responsible for keeping us alive.

I have always been amazed with how it functions. For example, why does it beat? Has anyone ever instructed his or her heart to beat? Of course not; yet day in and day out it beats. Why? That has always fascinated me.

Essentially, the heart is a pump. It is the muscle portion of this pump that does the beating. Like all muscles in our body, oxygen is the major fuel that allows it to perform its task. Without oxygen, the heart would be a pump without fuel. Think about the carburetor and fuel pump in your car. If it does not get the gas out to the rest of the engine, your car will not function. In the heart, the fuel is not gasoline, but oxygen. The heart pumps the blood out through the arteries to all of our vital organs so that they can function. It is that simple: We need the pump to keep working at *its* optimum so that we can live at *ours*.

The things that cause the heart to have problems are what I have spent many years as a physician studying. Which leads me to the reason for writing this book. After all these years of studying and observing, I have come to some life-altering and lifesaving conclusions about heart disease. I want to share with you my experiences and observations about the things you can do to keep your heart beating for at least 100 years. After 35 years of studying the heart, I am firmly convinced that this magnificent device is designed to last at least 100 years, if not longer. The problem is that few of us do the necessary things that will keep it in good working order for that long.

I have written this book in a way that will not be confusing. If I have learned nothing more in my years of practice, it is to communicate to my patients in *patient language*, not doctor talk. Together, we will examine all the factors that could influence your heart to develop problems. We'll look at the accepted, well-researched techniques for preventing heart problems, and we will also explore some of the newest concepts yet to come, some of which are still in the research stage.

We are living in a very exciting time; the advances in medicine, and specifically in the treatment of heart disease, are surfacing so rapidly that it is hard to keep up with them. That is another reason for this book. I want to keep you up to date. All of us, at some time in our lives, have dreamed about the possibility of living to 100. Our fantasy has us out playing tennis at 100, not sitting in a wheelchair in a nursing home. With the ongoing advances in medicine, the question I am frequently asked is, "How real is this dream?"

Since the number one killer in our nation is heart disease, this has to be the number one factor behind the dream of a long, healthy, and active life.

This book is going to look at the very real possibility of this dream becoming a reality. You will learn what factors negatively influence the heart. What you can do to alter these factors. I will also reveal the latest innovations in the field of nutrition and lifestyle changes. Many of the things you are about to read are based upon the latest scientific developments as published in recognized medical journals or presented at the most recent American Heart Association meetings. I will also use my 35-plus years as a practicing physician to evaluate these recommendations and share with you many of the conclusions I have come to based upon my experiences. My mission, at this stage of my career, is to share with as many people as I can what

I have learned from being in the trenches of primary care medicine.

I want to help as many people as I can to understand how the heart works and the things that can be done to keep it pumping for 100 years. The more lives I touch, the more content I will be.

Yes, I am hoping that this book is financially successful, and there is no question that was an important motivation for writing it, but above that I have been very fortunate to be able to spend so many of my years as a healer. I truly love how I have spent my life and would not trade one moment of it for another career. I now sincerely feel the time has come to give back. If this book can do that by helping you live longer, I will feel that I have accomplished my goal.

Finally, I have saved the *best* news for last. While the earlier you start the better, it's *never too late* to start. Soon I will be sharing with you ways to reverse the damage you might have already done.

In summary, this book can benefit everyone who is *still breathing*—young and old alike.

A physician should be trained to treat the patient and their disease, not just the disease that the patient has.

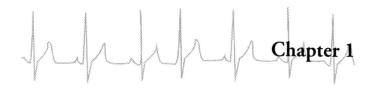

Chapter 1

ATTITUDE, SPIRITUALITY:
THE KEY TO LONGEVITY

You might think it strange that the opening chapter in a book about your heart is dealing with your attitude. But I must tell you that after 35 years of seeing patients, dealing with their minor or major problems, delivering their babies, operating on them and consoling families during terminal events, I have come to some significant conclusions as to the importance of the so-called mind/body reaction. To my amazement, I have seen two very similar patients with the same complaints, the same findings; diagnosed with the same illness and treated with the same medications, but each responded differently. One week after the start of treatment, one was feeling well, the other was still quite ill. This was not an isolated occurrence; rather, it has been an all too frequent one.

Yes, I realize people can have different reactions to medications, but it was more than that. Those who did better were different in their *response* to the treatment. Their whole demeanor was different. They were happy, often joking, and very positive in their overall attitude toward life. They did not obsess on their illness. They made light of it, while still doing the necessary things I outlined for them. They went on with their lives.

I have seen patients diagnosed with a terminal illness survive much longer than the medical specialists had anticipated. I have seen other patients with a minor illness become bedridden for several days. We all know people who get the common cold and do nothing but complain and suffer for the duration, while others simply ignore it and go on happily about their lives.

The question I've often asked myself, and now I ask you, "why?" What makes people react the way they do to health issues? Well, after all these years, I have come to the basic conclusion: *It's their ATTITUDE.*

I had the opportunity to address a large audience celebrating the 100th birthday of the Queen "Mum" of England. Several centenarians, born in the U.K. and living in the U.S., were invited as special guests. It is not often that we meet one person who has reached their 100th birthday; here in this audience were nine. When I was introduced, I mentioned to the audience that we were very fortunate to have this large group of centenarians with us.

I then asked if they would like to take advantage of this opportunity and have me ask each one of the centenarians, "What's the secret of your long life?" The word "Yes!" echoed throughout the auditorium. Next, I asked the audience to listen closely and see if there was some common thread in their answers. If so, we could all leave this event with some insight to living a long life.

I had already met each centenarian and already knew what all these elders had in common. But I was feeling rather chipper at the time and I wanted to have a little fun with the audience. One by one I asked each of the nine what their secret was—and I got nine different answers. At the end of the questioning, I asked the audience if they had heard any commonality.

A resounding chorus of "no" reverberated through the room. For each elder had given a very different reason. I announced that there was indeed one common theme. You could have heard a pin drop in that auditorium.

I waited a moment then said, "The common thread was not in *what* they said, rather in *how* they said it. Didn't you notice that when they spoke, each one of them had a very positive attitude? They were joking about their age. Not one of them dwelled about *any* illness."

One lady had said, "I had my breast removed when I was 75, but that was such a long time ago, I don't ever think about it." Another lady laughed and said, "I had half of my colon taken out because of cancer, but it weren't no big deal."

No matter what the medical history was—and they all had significant medical issues—they simply dealt with them and got on with their lives. They did not waste their time saying, "Woe is me!" or "Why me?" or "What did I do to deserve this?"

Then I asked the crowd, "How many people do we all know who dwell on their illness? Who spend their days talking about their failing health, the countless medications they take, and constantly spew their ongoing complaints and their persistent pains?" Every hand in the audience went up. I gestured to the nine proud centenarians and said,

"These folks did not do that. They have always had an exceptionally positive attitude about life. Their cups have always been half *full*!"

A huge round of applause rose up. After it subsided, I slowly scanned the audience as I said, "I am firmly convinced, and after this demonstration, you should be too, that a *positive attitude* is the primary factor in dealing with health issues. How you react to any illness, no matter how serious the diagnosis, is going to control how well you do in surviving that illness."

So what does the above story have to do with keeping the old ticker healthy and living to 100? It has everything to do with it. I will spend a lot of time discussing all of the standard scientific causes of heart disease: hypertension, cholesterol, cigarette smoking, etc. But I will also spend a substantial amount of time discussing the newly reported risk factors, such as anger, hostility, and negative thoughts. I have become very interested in the role of the brain and the effect of both positive and negative thoughts on health. The whole school of mind-body medicine is fascinating to me. The more I investigate, the more impressed I become with the significance of its role in wellness. Thinking your way to good health has recently been the topic of many research papers. As a matter of fact, there is a whole new school dedicated to psycho-neuro-immunology (PNI). More and more researchers are studying the role of thoughts and attitude on the body component responsible for keeping us healthy: the immune system.

Doctors like myself have long known that depression plays a very significant role as a cause of heart disease.

And it also plays a major role in a patient's survival *after* a heart attack. Those patients who are depressed after a heart attack, or after open-heart surgery, do not do so well as those who maintain a positive attitude.

Researchers at the Harvard School of Public Health have studied over 1,000 men in the Boston area from the Department of Veterans Affairs. The volunteers completed a questionnaire focused on determining whether they were basically optimistic or pessimistic. At the beginning of the study they were all reported as relatively healthy, with no known chronic medical conditions. The men were followed for an average of 10 years by questionnaire. Those in the study with the greatest degree of optimism had significantly less heart attack or angina (chest pain) history as compared to those with more pessimism or depression. This study was one of the first to document objectively, scientifically, the role of attitude in heart disease. Until then, most of the information was based upon nonscientific, or anecdotal reports. In a report released by the American Psychological Association (APA) in June of 2002, depression was reported to be linked to higher degrees of developing high blood pressure, having a heart attack, or dying after open-heart surgery.

Study after study is now linking the relationship between your attitude and your potential for heart disease and stroke. In following chapters we will evaluate the roles of anger, hostility, social isolation, and inability to cope with stressors as major factors in the overall health of your heart.

I will close this chapter by firmly stating: If you get nothing more from this book than the importance of maintaining a positive attitude, you will have accomplished a great deal toward having a *100-year heart*.

Question: What factors control your attitude? Answer: Your personality and attitude depend a great deal on your belief system. Your thoughts are directly related to your beliefs. If you are often depressed and speak negatively, your attitude will demonstrate that. Your body language will show that. When you think negatively, it only follows that you also behave negatively. And your body follows suit by having negative reactions to anything and everything. Changing that requires taking charge your personality. Making a conscious effort to become more positive in how you speak and act is the first step toward changing your attitude. For example, it is amazing how just a simple smile without needing a particular reason can affect your attitude, and hence your health.

You are in control of most of your behavior. Your thought processes set your attitude and actions. Things that happen to you or around you, and how you react to them, control your thoughts. Thus *you* are in control of your destiny!

What Role Does Spirituality Play?

"It is Part of the Cure to Wish to be Cured"

Recorded history documents that every culture has developed and used various techniques to assist those afflicted with illness. In every one of these cultures, some form of spirituality or prayer has likewise been documented as a potential tool for healing. If one defines spirituality as a belief in some entity greater than oneself, then spirituality can be traced back as far as the beginning of recorded history.

The Bible, and ancient Greek, Roman and Eastern cultures, all talk about calling upon a higher power for healing. Modern as well as ancient religion uses prayer as a healing tool. Early records of the Incas, the Mexican, Canadian, and American Indians document various chants and rituals for this purpose. So it should come as no surprise that for generations scientists have looked for evidence that prayer or meditation is beneficial.

Well, in the past several years, numerous papers have been published that demonstrate that those who pray do better with managing their illness than those who do not. Continuously, I have been amazed by how much better my patients do when they have strong religious or spiritual beliefs. Over years of taking care of critically ill patients, I have seen this time and time again. Whether they have just been diagnosed with a serious illness, or they have just undergone a major surgical procedure, those who regularly pray or meditate always do better than those who do not.

The whole concept of spirituality or prayer is based upon the ability to have a resource, of any type, that will calm. And to have a resource that can be called upon at any time. A technique that will provide, during moments of conflict, anxiety, or fear, a feeling of relief or of momentary peace. This feeling of peace is something that we all strive for, especially during those moments of sadness or grief.

Spirituality and prayer provide, to those who use it, a powerful tool for inner peace.

Meditation provides a similar response. During moments of deep meditation, the users are calling upon this tool to achieve a feeling of calm.

Researchers continually discover that those who use meditation also do much better after major surgeries. Logically then, one must conclude, that learning and using meditation or prayer is an important first step in the healing process.

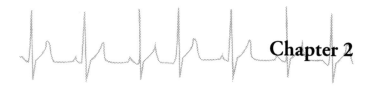

Chapter 2

WHAT HAPPENS WHEN YOUR HEART ATTACKS YOU?

Over the years, I have found that whenever I discuss medical subjects with my patients or with audiences, it is always helpful if we all are on the same page. As a reminder, the heart is essentially a pump, but not just an ordinary pump. It is the pump that's responsible for getting all of the blood around our body. It is without a doubt the most efficient pump ever designed.

Have you ever gotten up in the morning, stretched, and then said, "Good morning, Heart. Time to beat!" Of course not; we just take it for granted. In the normal body, this pump, on average, beats 70 times per minute. That's 4,200 times per hour, over 100,000 times per day, three million times per month...and we never think about it.

It is powered by a very efficient electrical system. An electric current is released in the upper chamber, transmitted to the lower chamber, and the heart beats. Like turning on a light switch. A rather important task, because the beating heart propels the blood that carries the oxygen—and all of our cells require oxygen to survive. If something were to interfere with this pump's function, naturally that would have significant repercussions.

Why is heart disease so potentially fatal? Well, if the pump in your car stopped pumping gas, your car would stop. If the heart does not pump blood to the lungs to get oxygen, and then on to the cells, they soon die and everything else stops as well. Obviously, for the sake of discussion, I have oversimplified the role of the heart, but trust me, as you read the following chapters you will appreciate my oversimplifications.

Unlike many of the self-help books I have read, I have no intention of overeducating you. For ease of understanding, whenever possible, I will give you the basic, necessary info to grasp a concept I feel is important for you to know. I realize that the simpler I keep things, the more inclined you will be to put them to good use.

For all you guys and gals who love to tear apart cars, and for the rest of us who just want knowledge, let's look at the miracle of the construction of the heart. Let me just interject something here (and I probably will mention this numerous times throughout the book): Our body is a miracle of construction. Without getting too religious on you, I must say that after dissecting the body and studying it for all these years, it is an unbelievable piece of work. Whatever the power or force that made us, it did a fantastic job.

Okay, back to the heart. To begin with, the heart is a muscular structure made up of four chambers. This big muscle is responsible for the pump's efficiency. The heart, about the size of a clenched fist, is located in the center of your chest. We always put our hand over the left breast when we salute the flag, and in doing so, we are off center by a few inches.

Coming out of these chambers are two major vessels: one artery (the pulmonary artery), and one vein (the pulmonary vein). Remember, the arteries carry the oxygenated blood around the body, and the veins bring it back to the heart and lungs to get more oxygen again and again. The one exception is in the heart itself. There, the artery carries the blood to the lung for oxygen, and then the vein carries the oxygenated blood back to the heart.

Connecting these chambers are valves that open and close each time the heart beats. Their function is to make sure the flow of blood is well controlled.

I am sure you have heard the term "heart murmurs." The murmur sound comes because the valve is not opening and closing well, and blood is leaking out. Fortunately, with today's sophisticated procedures, surgeons can replace these valves. As a matter of fact, there is a new procedure where the chest does not even have to be opened to replace a valve. A very fine catheter is fitted with a tightly rolled valve. This catheter is inserted into a vessel in the groin and slowly pushed upward to the heart. It is then directed, under actual visualization, to the diseased valve. The catheter is removed; the valve unrolls and stays in place. You just got a new valve. Again, a little oversimplified, but you get the idea.

Since this powerful muscle also needs oxygen to keep its cells alive, an MI, or myocardial infarction, (whoops, there goes one of those medical terms!) means the death of the heart muscle. We don't want that to happen: Hence the main focus of this book will be how to avoid this and other heart problems.

Let's get back to the question, "What is heart disease?" It's all about our arteries. Remember, they carry the blood, which contains the oxygen. If, for any of the reasons we will examine later, when we look at risk factors, the arteries clog or get full of "crud," the blood cannot flow through them. When this happens, oxygen does not get to the heart muscle, and boom- A heart attack or chest pain (angina).

The example I like to use involves a garden hose. You just went out and bought a new hose. You hook it up to the faucet, turn it on, and out comes this gusher of water. Twenty years pass; you turn on the hose and the water trickles out. If you were to cut open the hose, lo and behold, you would see that it is filled with crud and the water cannot get through. The same is true with your arteries. At birth, they are wide open, but after many years of doing lots of the wrong things, they too get clogged with crud—only we doctors call the crud "plaque." Like life itself, it's all about flow.

A good question at this point of the discussion is, "Are all arteries affected the same way—and how about our veins: Do they get the same *crud*? The answer to the first part of the question is *yes*. All of our arteries have the same potential of becoming clogged through the process of plaque deposition (I will go into more detail later when I discuss the new concept of inflammation). The crud, or plaque, is a fatty, yellowish material almost like Silly Putty. It collects on the lining of the arteries (doctor talk: the intima), only under specific conditions.

Those conditions occur because of all of the years of not taking good care of your heart. It comes from all the cheeseburgers, french fries, smoking, and all of the other bad things we do to ourselves.

Again, all of our arteries can become clogged and cause problems. The arteries in the heart, legs, the abdomen, the neck, and the brain are most at risk. When the clog happens in the brain, it's called a stroke.

The veins, on the other hand, are not as susceptible to plaque deposition and generally do not get the fatty material deposited in them. However, they are not free from problems. Veins have valves in them and these valves are responsible for bringing the blood back from the legs to the heart and lungs for oxygen. The reason for the valves is interesting. Gravity takes the blood in the arteries, away from the heart and down to the legs. But, how does the blood get back up to the heart? It has to go up against gravity. Every time the heart pumps, the valves in our veins open and close and bring the blood up in a silo effect.

Again, I don't want to get all religious on you, but I find this interesting: Since gravity was not reported till the 15th century by Newton, and we have been on this planet for thousands of years, how did the power or force that created us know about gravity? It had to know; otherwise we would not have the valves in our veins.

You may have heard that when a heart bypass surgery is performed, a vein is taken from the leg and is used to bypass the obstructed artery in the heart. Before that vein is put in place, it is turned upside down to take the valves out of play, since they are one-way stop valves.

I hope you'll excuse me for going off on an occasional tangent, but stuff like that fascinates me. In any event, back to clogged veins. That happens because either the valve becomes incompetent and can't pump the blood back up (varicose veins) or the flow slows down (for example, from sitting on an airplane too long) and clots form. You may have heard about people sitting in one position for too long and developing clots in their legs. We doctors call that type of clot a DVT, or deep venous thrombosis. For prevention, we strongly urge those who spend many hours on an airplane (or any long-time sitting position) to get up and walk around periodically.

A DVT can be dangerous because the clot may travel from the leg to the lung and cause a PE (pulmonary embolism...more doctor talk) or a stroke. This clot or embolism in the lung or brain is potentially fatal, since it cuts off the oxygen supply—and by now we know how important that is.

What is a Stroke?

A stroke is the result of either a clot or a hemorrhage in the brain or in the arteries in the neck leading to the brain. The clot is the result of the same process that happens in the arteries in the heart or legs. Yes, I am talking about plaque deposition. Again, the plaque causes narrowing in the vessel, which then blocks the flow of oxygenated blood to the vital cells in the brain, and they die. When this happens, and if a large enough area of the brain is involved, paralysis of the parts of the body controlled by this area may occur. There is also a situation in which only a small area of the brain is involved and only for a short period of time. We call that a TIA, (transient ischemic attack). Usually these do not produce permanent damage, but they may cause symptoms similar to a stroke that last for only a short period. It is not unusual for these to resolve in 24 hours or less.

Hemorrhage usually occurs when the blood pressure gets so high it literally causes an artery in the brain to explode. Fortunately, with today's medications, we do not see cerebral hemorrhages as frequently as we did years ago.

Another cause of hemorrhage in the brain is when an aneurism ruptures. An aneurism is a weakened area in the wall of the artery, similar to the bleb or blister that we used to see in the walls of the tube in tires. These usually occur because of a congenital condition (berry aneurism) or some other malformation at birth.

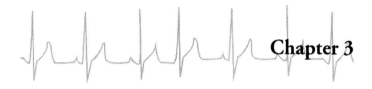

Chapter 3

HEART DISEASE IN WOMEN

I am including a special chapter on women because they have been left out on most discussions of heart disease—and also because of changes in statistics. Men, don't feel bad. Up until now, most books on heart disease were dedicated to you.

Until very recently, the number one killer of women was breast cancer. Most women thought of heart disease as a man's problem. That has now changed.

The number one cause of death in women is now heart disease!

The number one cancer-related death has also changed for women. It is no longer breast cancer. It is now lung cancer. Unfortunately, women, you have now joined men. Heart disease and lung cancer, are now the primary killers of both sexes.

I am firmly convinced that one of the major reasons for this is the fact that woman started to increase their use of cigarettes after the Second World War. Women left the home and started entering the workplace in much larger numbers. What previously was considered unladylike, smoking in public, has become an accepted behavior. With the birth of television, more and more women were seen smoking. Even one of the most popular TV shows, *I*

Love Lucy, showed the star, Lucille Ball, smoking. Movies also added to the problem, with female stars smoking in many of their scenes. It quickly became the norm for women to smoke just as much as men.

With this increase of tobacco use came its associated complications. This has been a slow process. It has taken 30 to 40 years for the end results to show up.

Based upon previous statistics demonstrating that heart disease was primarily a man's disease, and thinking that women were protected because of their estrogen production, many doctors failed to take a woman's complaint of chest pain seriously. Since it was rare to diagnosis a heart attack in a menstruating female, her symptoms were often ignored. Statistically, most heart attacks occurred in menopausal women (over age 45). The average age was 70.4; but that is all changing!

I have heard it said that the reason women were so frequently misdiagnosed was because they had different symptoms than men. They allegedly had what we refer to as atypical symptoms, as compared to the typical male complaints of chest pain radiating down the left arm. The atypical symptoms that were referred to included jaw pain, teeth pain, stomach pain, left wrist or arm pain. The facts are that men and women can both present with typical or atypical symptoms. It is not the symptoms that have caused us to misdiagnose women. It was our mind-set. Most doctors did not accept the fact that women were as susceptible to heart problems as men. Especially when you look at a woman's life span compared to that of a man's. Typically, when a menstruating woman would come into a doctor's office with a complaint of chest pain, many doctors immediately thought of chest wall, stomach, or emotional problems. Even when postmenopausal women came in, doctors were just not as sensitive to their complaints as they were to a man's.

Again, based upon a doctor's experience and teaching, women supposedly did not frequently have heart problems. I must share with you that in all my years of training and practice it was very rare to diagnose a heart attack in a woman who was still having her periods. Does that mean women were not having heart problems, or were doctors just missing the diagnosis? In the doctors' defense, coronary care units, the majority of times, were filled with men.

Just look at these statistics taken from the National Coalition for Women with Heart Disease:

- 8,000,000 American women are living with heart disease.

- 6,000,000 women have a history of heart attack or angina or both.

- 13% of women over age 45 have had a heart attack.

- 43% of deaths in American women occur from heart attacks.

Let's look at some other disturbing facts:

- Women who smoke risk having a heart attack 19 years earlier than nonsmoking women.

- 39% of Caucasian women, 57% of African American women, 57% of Hispanic women, and 49% of Asian women lead a sedentary life and do not get enough exercise.

- 23% of Caucasian women, 38% of African American, and 36% of Hispanic women are obese.

- High blood pressure is more common in obese women.

Now, do women have a right to complain that the medical profession is under treating them? Absolutely!

Look at these facts about women when compared to men and heart disease:

- Women are almost twice as likely as men to die after bypass surgery.

- Women receive less appropriate treatment.

- More women than men die each year from heart disease.

- Yet they receive fewer…

   a. Angioplasties and stents

   b. Bypass surgeries

   c. Implantable defibrillators

   d. Prescriptions for heart medications

e. And women comprise only 2.5% of participants of all heart research

Thus, the reason for this special chapter.

Ladies, the time has come for you to become PROACTIVE!

Based upon all we have talked about in this book, it is vital for your survival that you no longer sit back and say, "It is not going to happen to me."

Times have changed! Just look at the current statistics:

- The number one population in this country that has increased its smoking habit is females, and primarily teenage females.

- Anger and hostility are rapidly finding their way into the female personality.

- Coping is becoming a much bigger problem for women than ever before.

- Depression is much higher in women than ever before.

- Women today take more tranquilizers and antidepressants than ever before.

At this rate, will women continue to outlive men? Not likely. The gap is narrowing already. What will it be like in just 10 more years?

I recently attended a medical meeting where a new syndrome was discussed. The Japanese medical literature, a few years ago, started reporting what is now referred to as the *Takotsubo syndrome*, or the emotional heart syndrome. It was described as a group of heart-related symptoms, occurring primarily in postmenopausal women. They would get acute chest pain following an emotional experience. There are EKG changes and enzyme releases consistent with an acute heart attack. What makes this syndrome so unusual is that in reality, when their coronary arteries were studied by angiogram (injecting dye into them and taking movies of their function), no abnormalities were found. And in a couple of days, all abnormal findings were resolved, and there were no permanent changes.

What is fascinating about this is that more and more reports are appearing in the medical literature, and all of the cases occur in women. They seem to be directly related, or follow highly charged events such as having to speak in public, news-stimulated acute excitement, depression, major events such as earthquakes or floods, gambling, and rage. Several of these cases were identified in women in the San Fernando Valley of Los Angeles after the Northridge earthquake of 1994.

Well, the good news is...*it is not too late to change!* But you must become serious about addressing the problem. The first step is to identify your risk factors early. Be just as concerned as men when it comes to all of the things we are discussing in this book:

- Watch your diet, especially by eating more fish.

- Exercise as often as possible.

- Increase your intake of antioxidants.

- If you haven't already, stop smoking!

- Take the appropriate steps to deal with anger.

- Learn how to better cope, using meditation and/or yoga.

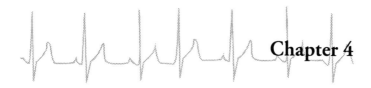

Chapter 4

WHY DOES OUR HEART ATTACK US?

I have often heard it said that man is a self-destructive animal. Most people spend the majority of their time on this planet doing things that will eventually end their lives. It is estimated that 70 to 80 percent of the illnesses we get are self-inflicted. We cause them by contamination of our environment and our counterproductive habits. We were given this magnificent gift, our bodies, and most of us are either consciously or unconsciously destroying it. When one stops to think of the numerous functions the body performs and the miracle of these functions, (here I go again) one has to be in awe as to how we were created.

I guess what I am trying to say is that the prime reason heart disease is the number one killer in this country is because of our detrimental lifestyles resulting from the self-destructive choices we make. We smoke, we eat the wrong foods, we do not exercise enough, we allow ourselves to grow fat, we are negative about many things, and we overreact emotionally.

We flat-out do not take care of ourselves. Most of us know better and we promise ourselves we are going to change. But making healthier choices is perpetually put off until a tomorrow that never arrives.

So here is a new concept that will work if you embrace it:

You go to the doctor, NOW—not later. He or she identifies your individual risk for getting one or more of the major diseases. You then take the necessary steps to deal with that risk. You now have an excellent chance of being able to prevent that disease.

This should be the main reason for *any* of us to go to the doctor. The annual physical should be dedicated to identifying your personal risk factors.

Based upon my experience with countless patients, I am firmly convinced that if *all* of us identified our risk factors for heart disease and then dealt with them, the epidemic of heart attacks (over a half million deaths per year) could practically be eliminated. One of the primary goals of this book is to inform you of these risk factors. This way, when you go to your doctor for your physical, you will know what has to be checked. I can't say it enough: *if you can establish your individual risk factors for any disease, and concentrate on dealing with those risks, you stand a good chance of being able to prevent yourself from getting those diseases.*

So let us now look at the risk factors for heart disease. These are the things you will want your doctor to check and discuss with you when he or she does your exam. I strongly urge you to take this list with you and make sure they all are checked.

(NOTE: There is a tear-out sheet at the back of the book that you can take with you to the doctor for your next exam.)

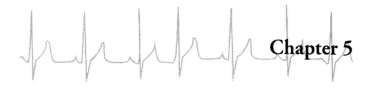

Chapter 5

THE TRADITIONAL
RISK FACTORS

- Elevated Blood Pressure (hypertension)
- Cholesterol

    a. HDL (high-density lipoprotein)

    b. LDL (low-density lipoprotein)

    c. Cholesterol/HDL ratio
- Lack of Exercise
- Smoking
- Diabetes
- Family History of Heart Disease Under Age 60

Hypertension

Number one on the list is high blood pressure. It's number one because statistically it causes more harm than all the others. Doctors call it the silent killer because most of us who have it don't know we have it.

So what is blood pressure? What are we measuring and why is it so important?"

We literally are measuring the amount of force it takes for the heart to pump the blood throughout your body. All pumps work against resistance. Whether it is the gas pump, the carburetor in your car, or the derrick pumping oil from the ground, they are pumping against some force. The less this force or resistance, the less work the pump has to do. The higher the force, the more the resistance, the more work the pump has to do.

As I mentioned, the heart is our master pump. It spends its entire life moving the blood around our body. So common sense will tell us that the less the resistance, the better it is for the pump.

Blood pressure measurement simply tracks how much pressure is required for the pump to get its job done. The higher the BP, the harder the heart has to work. The harder the heart works, the less efficient it becomes. The higher the pressure, the more strain is put on the arteries. If the pressure gets too high, the wall of an artery can literally rupture, just like a balloon with too much air. When that happens, we have a stroke.

Question: What does this all mean?

Answer: Well, we want to keep this pressure low enough to pump the blood to our vital organs including the brain and the kidneys. But not too low.

Question: What can cause low blood pressure?

Answer: Most commonly the cause is fluid loss or medication. Dehydration and blood loss deplete the fluid circulating in the arteries and this then decreases the resistance to the flow. The less resistance, the less pressure needed, and the lower the numbers.

I am often asked if the blood pressure can be too low. This question frequently comes from young women, since they often have low blood pressure. The answer is yes.

Generally, this is not a concern. It is not uncommon for some women to walk around with systolic (upper number) BPs below 100 (the norm is below 120).

The pressure must be high enough to get the blood to the brain and the kidneys. There are certain medical conditions where the BP drops so low the brain is not nourished and we have to give medications to raise the BP. We generally do not want the BP to drop below 80/60. By the way, the reasons young women have low blood pressure is because they are often mildly anemic due to heavy menstrual periods, and have a poor diet (iron-deficient). If the iron in their blood is low due to the anemia, and their pressure is not very high, they often complain of weakness, dizziness upon changing position (going from sitting to standing), and fatigue. This is easily corrected with iron supplements. Generally BP in the 90/60 range is not a problem.

Sometimes we are so concerned about elevated blood pressure we overmedicate and cause the decrease in BP. In addition to these causes, shock can also lower the BP.

We don't want it to go too high for obvious reasons. The normal levels for blood pressure have been established over the years by looking at thousands of readings and then relating the numbers to various medical problems, such as strokes, heart attacks, and kidney disease. The higher numbers (above 140/90) have been found much more frequently in patients with the above-mentioned problems.

By the way, you may have heard the terms "systolic" or "diastolic." (The 140 reading being the systolic, and the

90 being the diastolic.) These are terms referring to phases of the heart. When your BP is taken, a cuff is inflated on your arm. The pressure is released and the doctor listens with the stethoscope at your elbow. He is listening for the first sound that occurs as the pressure is released. This sound is the indication that the blood has started flowing through the artery. The pressure is noted and it literally is the pressure that it took to overcome the resistance of the occluded artery. When the sound stops, the vessel is completely open and this is the diastolic phase.

The reason you want your BP to be below 140/90 is that the lower numbers have been found in patients who live longer and have less disease. Some recent research is now suggesting that even the 140/90 numbers are too high and that normal BP should be below 120/80.

Now that you understand the numbers and what they mean, let's talk about *your* BP. If you have been told that your BP is high, were you told this after one reading, or have you had several readings? It is possible for all of us to have an isolated elevated reading. Even the healthiest and most conditioned astronauts have momentary elevations of their blood pressure just before liftoff. Before a diagnosis is made and treatment recommended, I suggest that you have your blood pressure checked at least *three times*. If it is elevated two of those times, that generally is sufficient proof for the diagnosis. Morning or afternoon readings in your doctor's office, separated by a few days, is my suggestion. Make sure that when your BP is checked that your biceps (upper arm) are at the level of your heart. This is best done with you sitting and your arm resting on a table. If you have a consistent elevation (over 140/90), I like to start therapy with what is called non-pharmacological treatment. This is a low-calorie diet, decreasing salt, increasing exercise, and incorporating relaxation training into your daily regimen.

Meditation has also been demonstrated to be a great "tool" for lowering blood pressure. I give my patients three months of the above therapy and if their BP is not reduced, then I am obligated to start drug treatment. The drugs we commonly use today fall into several categories, and your doctor will select one or a combination of them. They include diuretics, ace inhibitors, beta-blockers, calcium channel blockers, and alpha-blockers.

In the past, many of the medications produced significant side effects, so it's understood why so many patients stopped taking their pills. Remember, I mentioned most patients who have high blood pressure don't know they have it. They felt good till they started taking the pills and all of a sudden they felt bad. Fortunately, we now have available so many different and effective drugs, that should no longer be a problem, and no one should walk around with a high BP. If by chance you are taking one of the above pills and are having problems, let your doctor know *immediately*. With all the new varieties on the market, he or she should be able to find one that will be effective for you and have no major side effects.

As an aside, I am often asked, "How long should I take these pills?" My answer generally depends on your answers to two questions. (1) Are you having any side effects? And, (2) are the pills controlling your blood pressure? If the answers are no and yes respectively, I recommend staying on them as long as your doctor suggests. Everything we do in medicine is based upon the risk versus reward equation. If the reward far outweighs the risk, I say stay on them.

If you don't take them and your blood pressure goes up, you are a significant candidate for a heart attack, stroke, or kidney problems, and that will definitely take years off of your life.

I could not conclude this discussion of increased BP without the mention of "White Coat Hypertension." This very common reaction occurs every time some of us have to go see the doctor.

How many of you can identify with the following scenario:

To start with, you don't like going to see the doctor because you are scared to death about what he or she may find out. You come into my office and after some small talk, I say the following: "I suggest we check your blood pressure." Those words stimulate a mild panic. Even though it is a painless procedure, you get very nervous. I put the cuff on your arm, pump it up, and zing! Your blood pressure shoots way up. What did I do? I'm just trying to help you!

Here is another perfect example of how thoughts stimulate a chemical reaction in your body. For whatever the reason, you have been conditioned to fear having your BP checked. The thought stimulates the adrenal gland, it releases adrenalin (epinephrine), and up goes your BP.

The question that we doctors often have to deal with is, is this true hypertension?

What I do with my patients before I label them as hypertensive is have them buy a decent home-monitoring BP kit. I have them bring it into my office and I check it against mine for accuracy. I then teach them how to use it, and send them home with the instruction to check their BP morning and night for two weeks. Record the results and then come back to my office. I ask them to bring in a slip of paper with the results. The numbers usually are 118/68, 122/72, 124/70, all normal. I put the cuff on, 160/100. That's White Coat Hypertension. I follow up with these people every three months; have them start a low-calorie diet and an active exercise program. It is also very important that they get started on a relaxation program that includes meditation.

If you feel that you might have WCH, so that you are not misdiagnosed, I strongly recommend that you make the same suggestion to your doctor.

Reminder Question: What does our blood pressure tell us?

Reminder Answer: It simply measures the amount of resistance the heart is meeting as it pumps the blood out to the arteries. The higher the numbers, the harder the heart is working, the greater the risk for heart attack and stroke.

Cholesterol

Now that we understand the risks of high blood pressure, I want to discuss a risk factor that seems to cause more confusion than the IRS forms. How much have you heard about *cholesterol?*

What is it? When is it good for you? When is it bad for you?

What are so-called "good cholesterol" and "bad cholesterol?"

Recently, as if to add to the confusion, a popular best-selling diet book advocated eating as much fat as you want. Its proponents seemed to feel that fat in your diet is very beneficial. All the research by the American Heart Association and the American College of Cardiology strongly disagrees with that claim. As a matter of fact, one of the most extensive, if not the most extensive research into this subject, conducted in Framingham, Massachusetts, clearly indicates that increasing the fats in your diet plays a major role as a causative factor for heart disease. In addition, the American Cancer Society believes that fats are a factor in some cancers, including prostate, colon, and breast cancer. The population in Framingham has been under the scientific microscope for many years and the data accumulated has done much to impact the nationwide decrease of heart disease.

My advice is to avoid the fads. Stay with the scientific data and objectively controlled studies. If you seriously want to extend the life of your heart (say to 100), then you need to take a serious approach to reducing the intake of such high fat foods as...

- Cheeseburgers

- French Fries

- Ice Cream

- Red Meats

- High-Fat Dairy Products

A question I'm frequently asked is: "Why are elevated levels of cholesterol bad?"

First off, it is important to know that all of the comments I will be making about cholesterol and its potential for harm come from years of objective, scientific research. The data has been reported in numerous medical journals, including the *Journal of the American College of Cardiology*, and the *American Heart Association*. In addition to those prestigious publications, report after report from the 25 plus years of Framingham studies conclusively demonstrate that the higher the cholesterol, the greater the chance of a heart attack. So without further ado, and without getting too technical, let's take a look at what is going on...

Cholesterol is a very important material, and is the nucleus of several hormones. It enters our bodies two ways:

1. Your liver makes it, or

2. You eat it.

The amount the liver produces is directly related to your family tree, or your genes. In those fortunate ones, who have the "good genes," your liver only produces your body's minimally required amount. Therefore your blood level is low (or *serum level* as doctors call it).

The other way it enters our systems is in the foods we eat. Here is where the cheeseburgers, french fries and other fast foods cause problems. If, by chance, you are one of the lucky ones and you fall into the good gene category I just described, you can eat much of that high-fat food and still have low cholesterol.

As the process of metabolism goes on, all of the nutrients are transported around our bodies by the proteins. When a fat attaches to a protein to "hitch a ride" somewhere, we call that protein a *lipoprotein*. There are two different densities of these lipoproteins: a high density one and a low density one. We abbreviate them as HDL and LDL.

The HDL (high density lipoprotein) is the *GOOD* cholesterol.

The LDL (low density lipoprotein) is the *BAD* cholesterol.

Let's first look at the "good guy" HDL and find out why *it* is good.

The high-density component has the ability to protect the walls of the arteries from the deposition of the material that causes blockage and thus allows a normal flow of blood. Hence we call it the *good cholesterol*. We call this material "plaque" (no, it's not the same as the plaque on your teeth). Plaque is a fatty material that forms on the lining of the arteries as we age. When the artery is opened, you can literally peel this stuff out. Just like peeling silly putty from its mold. At this point in my talks, I am frequently asked at what age this plaque deposition starts. The answer: it starts young. Studies done on 18- to 20-year-old soldiers in Viet Nam, killed in combat, showed their coronary arteries were already loaded with plaque, which was restricting blood flow.

Every time you exercise, walk up a hill, run for the bus, or shovel the snow, you are putting greater demands on your heart to pump the oxygen to the coronary arteries. Think back on the old hose with no water getting through, this is the same thing that happens when your arteries clog up with plaque. Demand is made, the flow is decreased, thus the oxygen is decreased, and you have pain. We commonly refer to this pain as *angina*.

The other *lipoprotein* we are concerned about is the *Low Density* Lipoprotein (LDL). Here is where the trans or saturated fats come into play. They are directly involved in elevating the LDL or "bad cholesterol." In addition to the other foods mentioned, look carefully at the ingredients in crackers, cookies and other pastries. Trans fats are used to preserve them.

The LDLs are the "bad guys" because they are responsible for the formation and deposition of the plaque in the arteries, which then causes the arteries to become blocked and not allow the blood to flow freely, on demand.

"Triglycerides" is another term you will hear doctors use. These are also low-density lipoproteins, so I just group them together. The normal numbers for the "triglycerides" are the same as the other LDLs.

With this in mind, it should now make sense to want to keep your HDLs as high as possible and your LDLs as low as possible.(This is why it is so important for you to not get only your total cholesterol checked, but always include your HDL and LDL levels when you have your cholesterol blood test.) This test should always be done on a 12-hour fasting specimen so that recently ingested foods will not alter the results.

Let's now look at where your test scores should be, the normals:

TOTAL Cholesterol   200 mg. or below

HDL Cholesterol   45 mg. or higher

LDL Cholesterol   100 mg. or lower

Triglycerides   100 mg. or below

There is one additional set of scores you should ask your doctor to report to you. This is the HDL/Cholesterol ratio. Research at Framingham has clearly demonstrated that in addition to keeping your cholesterol scores within the recommended ranges, keeping your HDL/Cholesterol ratio low will also help protect you from getting heart disease. As a matter of fact, your ratio can predict your possibility, based upon population statistics, of having a heart attack.

The ratio is determined by placing your total cholesterol over your HDL cholesterol. By the way, the term "total cholesterol" is a misnomer. It does not represent the sum of the HDL and the LDL.

$$\underline{\text{CHOLESTEROL}} \quad \underline{200} = \text{RATIO: 4}$$
$$\text{HDL} \qquad\qquad 50$$

According to the Framingham studies, the lower the ratio the less the risk.

A ratio of "4" places you at average risk for a heart attack. A ratio of "2" places you at one half the risk. A ratio of "6" places you at twice the risk.

At this point I can imagine a reader thinking to him/herself, "Okay, that's great, so how do I lower my total cholesterol, raise my HDL and lower my LDL? Can I reverse the process?"

Those are excellent questions. If you cannot do something about changing your risk factors for disease, what's the point in learning about them? As I've mentioned previously, I will always give you a method of dealing with negative risk factors.

First let's deal with total cholesterol. There are two ways to deal with cholesterol problems:

1. On your own with proper diet and exercise

2. With help from your doctor with medication.

If you can do it on your own without medication, you are better off. This takes a mindset and often a lifestyle change. Remember, I previously mentioned that *because of genetics* some of us have livers that make more cholesterol than others. Well, if you fall into that category, you may not be able to do this on your own, but I certainly would give it the old college try. You must decrease the amount of saturated or trans fat you take in by diet. Yes, I am again talking about the cheeseburgers, the french fries, the ice cream, and all of those other junk foods our culture thrives on.

To demonstrate just how important your diet is, many studies have followed individuals from certain cultures and countries as they have changed their diet due to a change of location. One of the best examples of this is the first- and second-generation Japanese when they migrated to the United States. Their diet in Japan was based primarily on the intake of fish, rice, and soy products. When they left Japan and moved to America, they started eating more meat and dairy products with its associated saturated fats. Heart disease, which was not that common in Japan, suddenly became a significant cause of death in this U.S. population.

I recommend a diet made up of 25-30 grams of fat per day. Also I recommend that the fats in your diet be primarily unsaturated. Saturated or trans fats are the harmful ones. The difference has to do with whether they are liquid or solid at room temperature.

By definition, unsaturated fats are liquid at room temperature and are the ones that should be included in your diet. Olive oil is the one that I like the best, with canola oil running second. The exceptions to this rule are the so-called tropical oils, palm, cottonseed, and coconut oil. These are examples of liquid saturated fats. They are considered to be harmful, so I suggest that they be avoided.

Saturated fats on the other hand, are solid at room temperature. Butter, margarine, and lard are examples, and they also should be avoided.

There are several new solid spreads available. *Benecol* and *Take Control* are two examples. They are being promoted as being beneficial since they contain no trans fats. The jury is still out and we will have to see if they pass the test of time.

Measuring the amount of fat in a food is relatively easy today, since most products sold in supermarkets are labeled. Take a package off the shelf and turn it over. On the back will be a label describing the contents. Look for the *total grams of fat* per serving, not the percentage. If it indicates "10 grams of fat per serving" put it back on the shelf. If it reads "1 gram of fat per serving" *buy it*. Remember 25-30 grams is the *total* daily allowance.

Alternative Methods for Lowering Cholesterol

For years my patients have asked me about the role of the so-called "natural methods" of lowering cholesterol. Because everyone is looking for ways to improve their health, and because prescription medicines are more expensive then ever, over-the-counter or nonprescription herbal supplements are very popular.

If you recall, in the beginning of the book I mentioned that I generally do not recommend any treatment unless I have valid, scientific evidence that it will work, and most important, that it will do no harm.

In other words, I do not suggest treatments based upon anecdotal tales. The problem with most of these natural treatments is that there is little to no scientific evidence supporting that they work. I am sure that you do not want your doctor to recommend or prescribe a treatment or product that he or she is not familiar with, or that has no research to support its use. You especially do not want your doctor to prescribe something that potentially can produce problems. Without knowing the specific dose or potential complications, I could not in good conscience advise any of my patients to use an herbal product.

I am not saying that all of these herbs or natural medications are dangerous. I appreciate that some of them have been around for hundreds of years and that there is some research available that does indicate they may have value. The problem is that: most of these products are not regulated by the Food and Drug Administration (FDA). As a result, there is no standardization. The manufacturers are not obligated to guarantee the effectiveness, safety, or content of the product. Because of that, there are no *dosage standards*. In addition, many of them do not contain what the label indicates. Another problem is that some of them can interfere with medications you may be taking and produce side effects.

There are many different herbs available, but these are the ones that are promoted most frequently:

1. Guggulsterone (Guggul)
2. Policonasol
3. Capsicium
4. CoEnzyme Q 10
5. Chinese Herbs

My answer when questioned about the effectiveness of any of the above is: "I *hope* they do what they are promoted to do." Unfortunately, at this time, I just don't have any solid evidence that they actually do what the manufacturers claim. I would love to have scientific reports that support their use, but until I do, I cannot take them out of the anecdotal category.

I am sure you realize that I am always open to new information, but my primary responsibility as a physician is to do no harm and protect my patients.

One area that I am *very* supportive of is the use of foods to lower cholesterol. Here, since we are not dealing with drugs, and unless you have a specific food allergy, they will not cause harm. Thus I have no problem encouraging their use:

- Fish Oil (Omega-3s)
- Oatmeal
- Nuts
- Soluble Fiber (Psyllium)
- Garlic
- Soy Isoflavones

How Do I Raise My HDL?

Again, your doctor can play a very significant role with medication. We now have a new group of pharmaceuticals called statin drugs that are extremely effective in raising your HDL, lowering your LDL and total cholesterol. Brand names such as Lescol, Lipitor, Pravachol, Mevacor, and Crestor are a few examples. In addition to lowering cholesterol and LDL and raising HDL, statin drugs have demonstrated evidence of having a protective effect on the heart. In a future chapter I will be discussing the role of the new risk factors for heart disease. One of them is inflammation, and many researchers are suggesting that the statins may also be very effective in decreasing this inflammation, and are thus extremely beneficial as a preventative for all those with increased risk factors for heart disease.

Some of these drugs are not without potential side effects, so again the risk-reward ratio must be considered. One side effect is an elevation of the liver enzymes, which could indicate an inflammation of the liver. They also have been reported to cause a painful muscle condition in a few patients. Fortunately, this is not very common, and when the drugs are stopped the enzymes return to normal and the muscles heal. If this happens to you, your doctor may simply change the statin you are taking to resolve the problem.

Other cholesterol-lowering agents that have been around for some time include niacin and psyllium. Both of these are available without prescription. Recently, at a meeting of the American Heart Association, some very interesting observations were reported. In a study performed at the Walter Reed Army Hospital, one gram of niacin or a daily dose of psyllium (Metamucil) was added to the statin regime. What they found was a significant decrease in the LDLs with the psyllium and an elevation in the HDLs with the niacin. These changes were equivalent to doubling the dose of the statin drug and were significant because they decreased and slowed the progression of plaque deposition. According to Dr. Allen Taylor, director of cardiovascular research at Walter Reed, "Niacin is the most effective agent available for treating patients with low HDL levels." Since niacin can sometimes cause flushing or reddening of the skin, the patients were started off on low doses of 500 mg/day for 30 days and then elevated to the 1-gram maintenance dose. To help avoid the flushing, the patients were advised to take the niacin at night along with their aspirin.

Psyllium, which is commonly found in Metamucil, is a soluble fiber, which is frequently used to treat constipation or other GI problems. Doctors have suspected for several years that it also can lower cholesterol. Psyllium is very well tolerated.

In addition to these, there are two other ways that you can elevate your HDL:

A. Exercise, and are you ready…

B. *Alcohol!*

Yes, significant studies have demonstrated that exercise and 1 to 2 ounces of alcohol per day can increase your HDL by 15 to 25%. The reports discussed the intake of 1 ounce of spirits, scotch, bourbon, vodka, etc., or a 12-oz. glass of beer, or a 5-oz. glass of red wine. Now that does not mean that I am encouraging everyone to become an alcoholic. A patient of mine once asked, "If two drinks a day can increase my HDL by 15%, will four increase it by 30%?" Unfortunately the answer is *NO!*

The other frequently asked question is, "If I don't drink daily, can I save it up for a weekend binge?"

Sorry, I'm afraid not.

Additional studies have also shown that alcohol intake greater than two ounces/day has a significant impact on mortality. The risk-to-reward curve makes a sharp downward turn after two ounces, and the harmful effects from all illness and accidents increases significantly. Alcohol has produced many problems in our society and is not without risk. I want to make that perfectly clear. I am just reporting the facts about its effect on HDL. So please, always consider the risks versus the rewards.

How Do I Lower My LDL?

More and more evidence is now indicating that the LDL level is a very significant predictor of plaque deposition and heart disease. While a level of below 130 was the indicator in the past, doctors are now encouraging their patients to get the LDL to below 100 mg. As the opposite of the HDL, where the higher the better, with the LDL, the lower the better.

So how do we do that?

This is where eliminating the saturated and trans fats is very important. First and most important is a very prudent diet. If your LDLs are elevated, this is serious business. You want to decrease or eliminate as many saturated fats as possible. That includes all red and fatty meats, dairy products, fast foods, fried foods, and anything else with a high level of saturated fat.

In their place you increase the intake of unsaturated fats such as fish, skinless chicken, and nonfat dairy products. Salads, fruits, vegetables, and grains are also encouraged. And don't forget the foods that are high in antioxidants such as blueberries and nuts.

You may also want to take Metamucil (psyllium) on a daily basis.

If, after several weeks on this program, the LDLs do not come down, you should then begin a program of medication. Your doctor will prescribe what is best for you. All of the latest medical information now indicates that the statin drugs are the best to do this. Again, as with all medications, statins have some risk (elevation of liver enzymes and muscle inflammation), but I feel the reward far outweighs the risk.

Exercise

Yes, we finally got to that nasty word, but it is so important.

Worldwide studies have repeatedly shown that exercising is one of the most important things you can do to keep your heart healthy!

Every study reports two things:

A. All those who exercise, LIVE LONGER.

B. *Any* exercise is better than none.

Exercise…we all know it is good for you, but who has the time and motivation to keep it up? We all start out with great intentions. We join a gym, start jogging, or swimming, but pretty soon something comes up and we have to cancel our workout session. Before we know it we are canceling more than we are exercising.

Here's an interesting item that I recently came across: *A recent survey conducted on people who had bought a treadmill, revealed that they had purchased something else entirely. What they'd really bought was a very expensive clothes hanger!* Of course, I'm kidding! Unfortunately for many people, this joke is not far from the truth.

Most of us have been brainwashed to think that exercise means joining a gym and working out for two or more hours a day; or putting on our running shoes and jogging several miles. Put these thoughts aside. You do not have to run marathons or join a gym to get exercise. Yes, both of those are ideal forms of exercise. If you are the type of person who has the discipline to stick to a weekly exercise schedule, great! But understanding that *any* exercise is better than none means that you do *something* as opposed to sitting on your rear. I get so frustrated when I hear a patient of mine say, "I used to jog all the time, but now I am just too busy to exercise."

Here is a perfect example of what I mean: You go to the mall to shop for clothes. The parking lot is full. You drive around and around looking for that parking spot as close to the mall entrance as possible. Ten to thirty minutes may pass as you drive around, wasting your valuable time and most probably getting you aggravated. There are always plenty of empty parking places *far away* from the entrance. So *park there* and walk to the mall entrance.

That, my friends, is exercise. Yes, it's not the ideal exercise, but it is better than none. In addition, you are taking advantage of the time and you are saving yourself from the damage to your body caused by aggravation.

Another example I like to give involves the building your office may be in. If it has at least three floors, likely there will be an elevator. Consider this: Your building's elevator is primarily for the disabled or the very elderly. But you probably use it every day. However, unless you are disabled, or very old, why not *walk up the stairs?* THAT is exercise.

Even people with busy schedules can find time to exercise if they just use a little ingenuity. It actually takes *less* time to take the stairs (Consider how much time do you spend each day *waiting* for the elevator?). And, depending on how many steps there are, you may get a workout at least twice each day—and just by going to work, which you are doing anyway! See how easy it can be?

Now, I have to be a little careful here. One night my wife and I were having dinner and the phone rang. My wife answered and I heard her say, "Yes, Doctor Kornfeld is home. You want to speak to him about your husband? He's doing what? You better tell him!"

She passed the phone to me and I listened while a very upset wife reported that her husband had attended a talk I gave to a group of TEC International CEOs the week before. Based on my recommendation, he was not using the elevator, and at this moment he was walking up the stairs to his office, carrying his new computer. My immediate reaction was, "Good, what is the problem?"

She replied, "His office is on the thirtieth floor! He just called and told me he's halfway up and he is having chest pains." I responded, "I need to speak to him at once!"

She did a quick conference call, he got on the phone and his opening comment was, "Doc, I'm sorry, is my wife bothering you?"

"Absolutely not," I said. "Tell me what's going on." He repeated the story and added, "My chest felt fine until about the twentieth floor, then I almost dropped the computer."

First, I urged him to immediately seek medical attention. Then, I reminded him that I had specifically referred to an office on the *third* floor; and that with any new exercise, you start slowly and gradually build up to a higher level.

He, like most guys, wanted instant gratification. I guess it's a macho thing. We become weekend athletes and start at the marathon level instead of the beginner level.

The follow-up is that he saw his doctor; the searing pain was from his chest wall, not his heart. And he began *slowly* building up his exercise tolerance, walking up ten flights (sans his computer), then taking the elevator the rest of the way.

I am a frequent speaker for Vistage International. This is a worldwide organization of presidents and CEOs of large corporations. One of the most frequent comments I hear when I mention the importance of exercise is, "Doc, I used to exercise all the time. When I was in college I was an athlete. Now I am running a big company. I want to exercise but I just don't have time."

To that statement, I usually respond "Nonsense!" I remind them of a request that most of them made when they became president of their companies. I am sure you know that with the title of "President" comes with several very nice perks. One of those is the best parking space, you know, the one right in front of their office door with "Reserved for the President" painted on it. Is that really the best parking place? Absolutely not! Based upon "any exercise is good," it is the *worst* parking place. I suggest they give it to their most disliked employee. The best parking place is the one at the far end of the parking lot.(The one that requires you to *walk* as far as possible to your office.) That's exercise! Remember: "I don't have the time" is a poor excuse when you understand that *any exercise is better than none.*

I realize that we are all not going to become marathon runners, so let's look at what else is available to almost all of us:

Swimming, bicycling, jogging, and rowing if you are near a body of water, are all examples of good exercise.

I personally am a strong proponent of rapid walking. I like it because it is easy and inexpensive. Besides a good pair of walking shoes, you do not need any special equipment. You can do it anywhere and to me, most important is that it is a low-impact exercise. A recent survey in the UK reported by the British Heart Foundation found that citizens over age 65 who walked a minimum of three times per week lived longer than those who did not.

Low-impact exercise means that the forces of the exercise are not traumatic to your major joints. If you consider jogging, especially on blacktop or pavement, the forces directed to your hip joints every time you put your weight on your legs are tremendous. Multiply this force by the number of miles you run and you can understand why hip and back pain and its associated arthritis is a common complaint among marathon runners. In addition, if you were to look at the X-rays of the knees of retired basketball or football players, you will also see advanced arthritic changes.

I frequently counsel women to avoid high-impact exercise because their anatomy, and the structure of their pelvis, was designed to bear children, not to jog. Before I start getting mail from female athletes and marathon runners, I certainly am not telling you not to run. What I am saying is that with all activity, you must weigh the risks versus the rewards and go with what gives you pleasure. But please do so with moderation. I am also saying that there are other forms of exercise that are low-impact and will produce the same health benefits. In addition to walking, swimming is also a great low-impact exercise.

Okay, we discussed any exercise and its benefits; now let's look at ideal exercise. Here we are going to use your heart rate as a measurement of the so-called "physiologic, aerobic, cardiovascular exercise."

Aerobic simply means with oxygen, anaerobic means without oxygen. Usually an activity that causes your cardio-respiratory systems to increase its rate of activity and get more oxygen to the tissues is considered aerobic.

The question now arises as to the frequency and length of time necessary to accomplish a good aerobic, cardio-vascular workout. The first thing we want to do is establish a target heart rate that you should strive for. This rate will be based upon your age. To do this we use the following formula:

220 minus your age (this number was calculated by exercise physiologists)

As an example, let's say you are 50 years of age:

220 – 50 = 170

That means, at age 50, your target heart rate is 170 beats per minute if you exercised at 100% of maximum.

Most cardiologists and exercise physiologists, however, prefer that you do not exercise at the 100% level. They prefer exercising at the 80% level. So you multiply 170 x 80% and you get 136 (I would round off the number to 140).

At age 50 an ideal program for cardio-vascular aerobic exercise would be to get your heart rate to 140 beats per minute (80%). You want to keep it at this level for a minimum of 20 minutes, three times per week. The idea is to have a continuous, non-intermittent program. For example, tennis and softball are great sports, but they involve a lot of stopping and starting.

As with all other programs, build slowly. The problem with getting your heart rate up too rapidly is that you may cause some alterations in the rhythm, or as we doctors call it, an *arrhythmia*. Generally these do not cause problems, but they can. So I suggest, if possible, avoid exercising at 100% of maximum. The chances are pretty good that if you have not exercised in a while, the heart will start beating rapidly very soon in the program. This indicates that you are out of condition, and is another reason to start slowly.

If you are in great shape and run marathons or get plenty of exercise, your resting heart rate is probably in the upper 40s or low 50s. The chance of getting your heart rate up to that target level is very slim. The heart muscle in marathon runners is in such good tone that it can accomplish the same work with much less effort. In addition, if you take certain medications for blood pressure or heart problems, like beta-blockers, you also will have difficulty increasing your heart rate.

A good way to monitor your pulse rate is with instruments or gadgets that you can get at most exercise stores. Or you can simply count your pulse rate. I recommend the carotid artery, which is the artery in your neck under your jaw. It is easier to check this artery while you are exercising than the pulse in your wrist. Simply use the first two fingers of your hand, place them under the angle of your jaw, under your ear lobe and feel the heart beat. Count how many times it beats in ten seconds, and then multiply that number times 6 and you have your heart rate per minute. For example, if you count 15 beats in ten seconds and you multiply that by 6, your heart rate is 90.

In summary, establishing your target heart rate, and exercising to it for 20-30 minutes three times per week, is the optimal program. Strive for it. But don't forget: *Any* exercise is better than none.

One word of caution, these recommendations are for asymptomatic, healthy individuals. Always check with your doctor before you start any exercise program.

Smoking

There is absolutely no question about the role of smoking and its effects on heart disease. Do you remember that the Surgeon General's warning on the packs of cigarettes used to say "may cause" cancer or heart problems. Well those "maybe" days are over. Cigarette smoking *does* cause cancer and heart disease.

Most smokers know the risk. They have heard it from doctors, their family members, and their friends. What motivates people to behave in certain ways has always amazed me. I have visited numerous patients in the coronary care unit after having a massive heart attack and almost dying. At that moment they all make the same statement.

"Doc, thanks for saving my life! I realize now how bad those damn cigarettes are, and I am done with them for good."

I congratulate them on their very wise decision. Then, six months later they are back to smoking.

I appreciate how difficult it can be to stop because smoking creates a physiologic addiction to nicotine. That means your body needs it.

Stopping, as with all addictions, is very difficult. Symptoms of withdrawal, depression, and tingling around your mouth and extremities commonly occur. Tools such as patches, pills, and gum are available. Unfortunately they do not work for all. But if you take the time to experiment, you'll find what works best for you.

I urge you to take this moment and consider the effect smoking has on your heart. If you are not motivated to do it for yourself, seriously consider how your quitting (or not quitting) will affect your loved ones. Please take yourself out of the picture and ask, "How will the people I love feel when I am bedridden with only a few months to live, and unable to be there and enjoy life with them?"

My advice, understanding the frustrations, is to:

1. Decide you're going to stop.

2. Get whatever help you can from the pills, patches, and gums.

3. Get as much support as possible from loved ones.

4. Think of your family members, especially your kids, and the harm you're causing them from second-hand smoke.

5. Then STOP (yes, cold turkey).

One of the other major problems with smoking besides cancer and heart disease is emphysema. This is a horrible disease. After many years of smoking, the lungs cannot function properly and you cannot breathe. You die a tortuous death, as the great entertainer, Johnny Carson, experienced. You literally suffocate to death.

And finally some good news, the younger you are when you stop, the greater the chance of reversing the process.

Diabetes

Uncontrolled diabetics have a significant increase in heart and other vascular problems. A diabetic's primary difficulty is that the cell in their pancreas (beta cell) that is responsible for producing the hormone insulin is "broken." The normal fasting blood sugar is between 70 and 110. When the non diabetic eats a meal with increased sugars (calories), the blood sugar goes up. This then stimulates a thermostat-like receptor in the pancreas that regulates the release of insulin. Its job is to keep the blood sugar level in this normal range. So it releases insulin in an amount necessary to get the blood sugar back to this normal range. When the diabetic eats foods high in sugar and their blood sugar goes up, minimal to no insulin is released, and the result is diabetes.

The question I always asked my professors in medical school was, "Who set this thermostat?" Another example of the miracle of our body!

Diabetes is divided into two types:

Type 1, Insulin Dependent Diabetes (IDD)

Type 2, Non-Insulin Dependent Diabetes (NIDD)

Type 1 (IDD) is usually associated with an onset in childhood and may be a little more difficult to deal with. However, it may occasionally begin in adulthood. Usually there is a strong familial or genetic predisposition. With IDD, the patient is required to take injections of the hormone insulin because certain cells in their pancreas are not producing it in sufficient levels to keep their blood sugar normal. Diabetics usually can live a perfectly normal life as long as they can keep their blood sugar levels in a reasonably normal range. This is becoming easier and easier as newer methods become available for getting the insulin into the system. Insulin pumps, inhaled and sprayed insulin are the newest methods to replace the traditional injected mode. The other most important part of the treatment regime is DIET, DIET, and DIET.

Diabetic diets take into consideration the amount of insulin the patient takes daily. These are usually based upon the amount of calories the patient needs on a daily basis. This is calculated based on weight and activity. The lower the caloric intake the better.

One of the major problems a diabetic can have is not adjusting their insulin dosage to their caloric intake. If they take too much insulin and lower their blood sugar *too* low, they become hypoglycemic. The reverse of that is not taking enough insulin, and the blood sugar goes up. Both of these conditions can produce serious complications, coma being one of the most serious. It's these alterations that cause both the patient and the doctors the most concern.

The persistent elevation of the blood sugar can cause problems such as…

- Inflammation of the blood vessels

- Heart disease and stroke

- Poor healing

- Kidney disease

- Vision problems

- And in severe cases, coma

Monitoring daily blood sugar is the best way to control diabetes. Dosages are adjusted based upon the numbers.

Type 2 or (NIDD) often starts in adulthood and is frequently associated with obesity. Here the primary treatment is DIET, DIET, and DIET. There are also oral medications that Type 2s can take to help keep their blood sugar levels in the normal range. Since they generally are not taking insulin, the potential for drug-related complications are less.

In both type 1 and type 2 blood sugar control, weight reduction and exercise play a very important role in keeping you free from vascular and heart disease and their complications.

Unfortunately, due to the current epidemic of obesity in children, we are seeing an increase in diabetes in teenagers. Therefore, I strongly urge you to take a very concerned interest in your kids' diets, as well as your own.

Family History

There is no question that our genes control much of our destiny. But as I often say, how you treat your genes also plays a very important role. I like to give the example of two chefs--one is fantastic and the other is horrible. You give them both the best ingredients and ask them to prepare a meal. The great chef turns out a magnificent feast, the bad chef turns out a lousy buffet. Similarly, while good genes do play a role, your lifestyle also is very much involved.

One of the first inquiries your doctor may make when doing your exam is about your family history. We are very concerned about the health of your parents and grandparents. A history of diseases such as diabetes, depression, some types of cancers, and heart disease can be important in making future diagnoses.

If you have a strong family history of having a mother, father, or grandparents with any of the above diseases occurring under age 60, there is a significant risk that you might also be a candidate. It appears that the age of onset of the disease plays a major role in the genetic predisposition. Heart attacks tend to be more common in those with a strong history.

When I discussed risk factors for heart disease, the majority of them were something you could change. Family history is the one risk factor you cannot control since, as of this time, we do not have the ability to alter genes.

But that said, I am not as concerned about family history as I once was. Here is the reason why: Let's say your father had a heart attack at age 52. At that time, doctors were not as concerned with the risk factors as we are today. Your father may have been a smoker with high blood pressure and elevated cholesterol and LDL cholesterol prior to the attack. If we had the information back then that we have today, and he was told about his risk factors and did something about them, he may very well have been able to avert the heart attack.

This is not to say that I am not concerned about family history at all. I still am, and I will pay more attention to your symptoms, based on the history. What I emphasize is that those with a family history of heart problems should be extra diligent in getting their risk factors checked and taking all the necessary steps to control them. *If you do, and you control them by following the program outlined in this book, there is a good chance you will not become another heart attack victim.* And who knows, you may very well be able to alter your family tree.

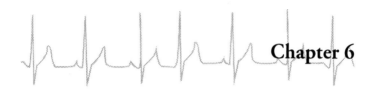

Chapter 6

OBESITY & WEIGHT LOSS

Since obesity is a significant risk factor for heart disease, I want to spend some time clarifying the mystery of dieting. So many of us spend our lives as obesity yo-yos. We go up and down.(Gain weight, lose weight.)

Over the years, I have been asked many times about various fad diets. I have been in practice long enough to have seen hundreds of different diets come and go. What all fad diets have in common is that they are just that, a passing fad. A new book promoting a particular type of diet regimen is published. The author is invited to appear on the major talk shows to discuss his or her revolutionary new diet. It is the subject of conversation at cocktail parties. Everybody is suddenly losing weight on this fantastic, new diet. That lasts from 6 months to a year before the next hot diet book comes out.

As I said, I've seen them all, from the water diet all the way up to the Atkins diet. To me, the weirdest one of them all was the HCG diet. HCG stands for Human Chorionic Gonadatropin. This is the material that is secreted in the urine of a pregnant female. As a matter of fact, that is what we test for when we do a pregnancy test. Well one of these diet gurus touted HCG as a weight-loss miracle. Take it and weight loss is guaranteed. Suddenly, thousands of overweight patients were coming into doctors' offices wanting to get injections of pregnant females' urine. Who knows how much they had to pay for this bizarre diet fad.

One day, a regular patient of mine was in my office for her annual physical and she happened to mention that she was getting these shots. I could not believe what I was hearing. She told me that she got them *three times a week,* and yes, she was losing weight. When I questioned her further and asked if she was on any kind of dietary restrictions, she responded, "Oh yes, he has me on a five-hundred calorie diet." Hello! Of course she was losing weight, and it had nothing to do with the HCG. She was losing weight because of the restricted *500 calorie* intake.

Let's get clear once and for all: Weight loss or gain is directly related to the *calories* you take in. Regardless of what a diet fad is preaching, you will lose or gain weight if you either decrease or add calories. It is that simple! The basic principle of weight control is based on the concept of calories in or calories out. The reason many of these fad diets *seem* to work is that when you say you are on a diet, regardless of what name you call it, you are consciously thinking about what you are eating. You are actively trying to control your weight. You have a much better chance of taking weight off when you are conscious of calories, than you do if you are not paying attention to what you eat.

So here is the principal: Your body requires a certain amount of calories for you to function. Calories are a unit of measure. They are what your body uses as fuel for you to do your daily activities. If your basic maintenance level (the amount you need to do all of these activities) is 2,500 calories, and you take in through the foods you eat 3,500 calories, you have ingested 1,000 calories more than you need. It would be wonderful if our bodies could say, "Sorry, I don't need that extra 1,000 calories, so let's get rid of them." If this were the case, we would never gain weight. But our body is always preparing for an emergency. What happens if we can't get food for a period of time? Well, the body takes that extra 1,000 calories and stores it in the "bank" and we gain weight. The bank, in this case our fat depots. It is there waiting for the emergency. On the other side, if you take in only 1,500 calories and you need 2,500, the body goes into the bank and withdraws 1,000 calories and we lose weight. It is that simple: Calories in, calories out.

With an understanding of the role of calories in weight control, there are two things that you can do to lose weight: Decrease the amount you take in or be more active and burn more.

Now that I have explained the role of calories and you understand that dieting is directly related to the calories you ingest. Everything should be simple enough, right? Unfortunately in the real world, calorie counting is almost impossible. Unless you have a full-time nutritionist counting for you, it is very difficult. But don't feel bad, help is on the way. The following guidelines have just been produced by the federal government and hopefully they will make it easier.

These guidelines reemphasize the need for controlling calories. Just as I have advised, they strongly suggest that your caloric intake should be directly related to your activity levels.

They separate activity into three categories:

Sedentary: light physical activity.

Moderately Active: walking one mile/day.

Active: physical activity equivalent to walking more than three miles/day at a rapid rate.

The daily caloric need for each category is as follows with the lower number for females

Sedentary	1,800 to 2,200
Moderately active	2,200 to 2,600
Active	2,200 to 3,000

After years of trying to get my patients to count calories and watching them become frustrated in the effort, I resorted to the age-old adage, "Keep It Simple!"

Since most doctors believe that fat is the enemy and that many of the calories people take in are from fats, we could help our hearts and our waistlines by controlling their total intake. I suggest that instead of trying to count calories, just be concerned with the *types* of food you ingest. Decrease the sugars and the fats and increase the vegetables, salads, fish, and fruits.

The reason many people lost weight on the recent carbohydrate fad is that they are primarily high in calories. Carbohydrates are divided into two classes, simple and complex. The simple carbohydrates are the sugars. The complex carbohydrates are the starches: potatoes, rice, bread, etc. By decreasing carbs you are, in effect, decreasing voluminous calories and you lose weight. The only difference with this diet is that the food industry smelled "Big Bucks" and made "low carbs" into a fad. Based upon my years of experience with fad diets, I predict that the low-carb foods will be history within the next five years.

Here is what the new guidelines suggest should be included in a 2,000 calorie diet on a daily basis:

- Veggies…five servings (2 and 1/2 cups) per day

- Fruits…four Servings (2 cups)

- Grains…six servings (six ounces), 1 cup cereal, 1/2 cup rice, or pasta

- Protein…five and 1/2 ounces (all fish, skinless chicken, or lean meats)

- Dairy…three cups (nonfat products)

- Fats…20 to 30 % of calories (unsaturated)

- Alcohol…Women: one drink/day;
    Men: two drinks/day
    (a drink is one ounce)

- Sodium (salt)…one teaspoon

Body Mass Index (BMI)

By the way, the new method being used to establish obesity is called the *Body Mass Index* or BMI guide. Doctors are no longer using just your weight as the indicator. BMI measures your weight and height, and using a formula, comes up with a recommended chart. Normal BMI is below 25.(Over that is varying degrees of obesity.) Insurance companies are now adjusting their actuarial tables according to BMIs.

Risk of Associated Disease According to BMI and Waist Size

BMI		Waist less than or equal to	Waist greater than
		40 in. (men) or 35 in. (women)	40 in. (men) or 35 in. (women)
18.5 or less	Underweight	—	N/A
18.5 - 24.9	Normal	—	N/A
25.0 - 29.9	Overweight	Increased	High
30.0 - 34.9	Obese	High	Very High
35.0 - 39.9	Obese	Very High	Very High
40 or greater	Extremely Obese	Extremely High	Extremely High

Determining Your Body Mass Index (BMI):

The table below has already done the math and metric conversions. To use the table, find the appropriate height in the left-hand column. Move across the row to the given weight. The number at the top of the column is the BMI for that height and weight.

BMI	19	20	21	22	23	24	25	26	27	28	29	30	35	40
Height (in)							Weight (lb.)							
58	91	96	100	105	110	115	119	124	129	134	138	143	167	191
59	94	99	104	109	114	119	124	128	133	138	143	148	173	198
60	97	102	107	112	118	123	128	133	138	143	148	153	179	204
61	100	106	111	116	122	127	132	137	143	148	153	158	185	211
62	104	109	115	120	126	131	136	142	147	153	158	164	191	218
63	107	113	118	124	130	135	141	146	152	158	163	169	197	225
64	110	116	122	128	134	140	145	151	157	163	169	174	204	232
65	114	120	126	132	138	144	150	156	162	168	174	180	210	240
66	118	124	130	136	142	148	155	161	167	173	179	186	216	247
67	121	127	134	140	146	153	159	166	172	178	185	191	223	255
68	125	131	138	144	151	158	164	171	177	184	190	197	230	262
69	128	135	142	149	155	162	169	176	182	189	196	203	236	270
70	132	139	146	153	160	167	174	181	188	195	202	207	243	278

BMI	19	20	21	22	23	24	25	26	27	28	29	30	35	40
Height (in)							Weight (lb.)							
71	136	143	150	157	165	172	179	186	193	200	208	215	250	286
72	140	147	154	162	169	177	184	191	199	206	213	221	258	294
73	144	151	159	166	174	182	189	197	204	212	219	227	265	302
74	148	155	163	171	179	186	194	202	210	218	225	233	272	311
75	152	160	168	176	184	192	200	208	216	224	232	240	279	319
76	156	164	172	180	189	197	205	213	221	230	238	246	287	328

Body weight in pounds according to height and body mass index.

As to specific diets, remember the LDLs and triglycerides are the bad guys. You want them to be as low as possible. The best way to control these would be the same as controlling your total cholesterol. Decrease the fast foods, the animal fats, the fried foods, the dairy products, and the sweets. Red meats like steak and hamburger are tender due to marbling.

That's the fat that you see streaking across your steak. The more the marbling, the more the saturated fat, and unfortunately for meat lovers, the more tender the meat (choice or prime). If you really love a good steak, I am not going to tell you not to have it. After all, we only live once. But I do ardently recommend moderation. So I suggest that if you choose to eat red meat, at least cut it down to once every two to three weeks, instead of every night.

I am a strong promoter, as is the American Heart Association (AHA) of fish as the primary source of protein in your diet. Studies presented at the 41st annual meting of the AHA demonstrated that eating fish at least once per week was associated with a significant decrease in heart attacks. Additional research has shown that in older individuals there was a 44% lower risk of dying from a heart attack in the group that ate fatty fish at least once a week. It seems that this benefit is coming from a material called omega-3 fatty acids. This is a very potent antioxidant and is present in higher quantities in fatty fish. Therefore the idea then is not only to eat fish, but to eat fatty fish. Salmon is the best example of a fatty fish.

More and more research is now telling us that a diet high in fish, by itself, may be responsible for decreasing mortality from heart attacks and stroke.

A recent report published in the Archives of Internal Medicine showed that those men who ate the good fats, (unsaturated fats such as omega threes in fish) were 60% less likely to die of heart disease than the men who ate the least amount of these fats. The study involved over 1,500 men living in Finland and lasted over 15 years.

Fish, Fish, Fish and their omega threes, I can't say it enough! They play a very powerful and important part in *increasing* the life of your heart!!!

YOU MUST INCLUDE FISH IN YOUR DIET!

Now that you got the message about fish, I have a word for those of you who hate fish. The recommended intake of omega-3s is at least 1-2 grams per day. Well, for you non-fish eaters who want another way of getting your omega-3s, there's a new prescription medication called OMACOR.(It was recently approved by the FDA,) and it will deliver the recommended dose.

There are also fish oil products sold without prescription. Unfortunately, as with any medication, there is some risk. For those taking anticoagulants there have been some reports of prolonged bleeding.

Here are some examples of the omega-3 content in a 3-oz. serving:

Salmon.. 1.8 gms

Herring .... 1.8 gms

Halibut .... 1.0 gms

Pollock .... 0.46 gms

Shrimp .... 0.27 gms

Lobster .... 0.41 gms

Flounder .... 0.43 gms

*Shark .... 0.90 gms

*Albacore Tuna (canned) .... 0.73 gms

*Swordfish .... 0.70 gms
*(higher in mercury)

As far as the mercury content is concerned, I think in general the benefits and rewards from eating fish far outweigh the risks.

However, the FDA recommends that women who are pregnant, planning to become pregnant, or nursing, and young children, should not eat the fish high in mercury. But they certainly can eat the other fish.

As you can see, we are now recommending that you eat *all* fish, including shellfish. I know we used to tell you not to eat shrimp or other shellfish because of cholesterol. Well, the latest thinking is that the fat in fish is the good fat. It is mostly polyunsaturated and it is so high in omega 3s, that the benefits far outweigh the risks.

To me, salmon is the best. It is very fatty and great tasting, especially when fresh caught and grilled. I know that there is some controversy over the farm-raised versus the wild. All of the reports I have read do not indicate that this is a problem, especially when you (again) weigh the risk to the reward.

Chicken and turkey are also good sources of protein. But you have to be careful of chicken because it too contains a lot of saturated fat. The chicken or turkey breast with all of the skin and fat trimmed is acceptable.

And *no*, you cannot *fry* the fish or chicken in olive oil. Once you fry anything, the fat becomes saturated. And I know you remember, "saturated fat is a no-no." So grill it, bake it, barbecue, or roast it.

In summary, the one diet that I am a strong proponent of is the Mediterranean Diet, because it includes the following:

- Fish

- Salads

- Vegetables

- Fruits

- Grains

- Pasta

- Water

And to finish it all off...a nice Chianti.

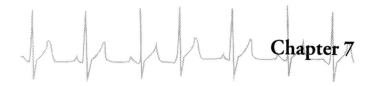

Chapter 7

THE FAST-FOOD INDUSTRY

S ince we are talking about obesity, and since the fastest growing and number one population affected by this epidemic is our children, I think that is important to include a *PLEA* to parents, food companies, and fast- food restaurants to become proactive and help stop this epidemic.

Any discussion of keeping the heart alive longer has to consider the role that society plays, and especially the foods that a culture ingests, as part of the discussion. Since it is my goal to keep as many hearts alive as possible to age 100, I would be remiss if I did not direct a part of this book to the role the food industry plays. We are all victims of the foods that are promoted and sold in our grocery stores and our restaurants. For example, early on in this book I mentioned the change that occurred in the rate of heart disease in the first and second generation Japanese after they moved to the U.S. and took on our standard diet. Heart attacks and deaths increased significantly.

Recently, I was most impressed after reading about the impact a physician, Pekka Puska, M.D., had on reducing the mortality and occurrence of heart disease in his native Finland.

Finland had far and away the highest coronary heart disease mortality in the world. Yet, with his efforts and drive, and with much to their credit, the cooperation of the global food companies, he was able to reduce the incidence by 82%. The project that he was in charge of took 30 years to accomplish and it is still working diligently.

We in this country are in the midst of an epidemic. It is not bad enough that heart disease is the number one killer of our citizens, men and women alike, decimating over 500,000 of us annually, but we are also in the midst of an obesity epidemic. And the sad part is that our teenagers are right in the heart of it.

This obesity issue is due to two things: lack of exercise and poor diets. Many school athletic programs have been eliminated and the average teenager spends the majority of his or her time in front of the TV or the computer. If that is not bad enough, the ads they see and hear promote outrageously bad, unhealthy foods. I feel strongly that the entire fast-food industry has to be held responsible for their outlandish encouragement of high-calorie, high-fat foods. It seems that the fast-food restaurant chains are only concerned with profits. When are the parents, health educators, and politicians going to become concerned? Is it going to take a major crisis? The time has come for the media to stop looking at the bottom line. They've begun to do it with tobacco and alcohol. When are the food giants going to realize that they can also make a very nice profit with foods that are healthier?

I was shocked when I saw the new product a national fast-food restaurant recently came out with. An average one of these hamburger monstrosities contains over 1,400 calories and well over 100 grams of saturated fat. Add to that a bag of fat-soaked french fries, a chocolate shake, or a sugary soft drink. Who can question why we are having this epidemic? I feel it is time for me as a parent, grandparent, physician, and author to yell and scream about this outrage! It is also time for everyone reading this book, who wants their kids and grandkids to live to 100, to yell and scream too. Early in this book I said that we humans are self destructive. Well here is the perfect example.

My message to the food industry:

STOP KILLING US—AND ESPECIALLY OUR KIDS!!!

- Learn from the Finnish experience.

- Become a part of the solution not a part of the problem.

- Produce healthy foods.

The global food companies that were involved in Finland learned that they could still make large profits at the same time that they helped to resolve the problem. I understand that several of the giant food companies are now "trying to help" with production of foods lower in calories and fats. Unfortunately *trying* to help is not the same as an all-out effort. Physicians and health educators all over this world are doing everything they can to eradicate heart disease, our primary killer. Emphasis on eliminating the risk factors is definitely helping. But we cannot do it alone. We need everybody's 100% dedication.

It is amazing how rapidly low carb foods appeared on the store shelves when the manufacturers were threatened. We can solve the problem. We can live to 100. And here's how:

- Parents: Stop buying unhealthy foods for your children.

- Food companies: Become PROACTIVE, produce low-fat products. Stop using trans fats.

- Fast-food restaurants: Please serve healthier foods.

- The last step…legislate changes, support and pass new laws to protect our children.

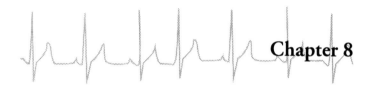

Chapter 8

THE NEW RISK FACTORS

Traditionally, when we looked at an individual's risk for getting a heart attack, we looked at their blood pressure, their cholesterol, their HDL, nd LDL. We asked if they smoked, had diabetes or a family history of heart disease. Statistically those factors accounted for about 75 to 80% of the heart attacks we diagnosed. But what about those who do not have these risk factors; do they ever get a heart attack?

For years doctors have been confused when certain patients came into the emergency room with chest pain. They have all of the signs and symptoms of a heart attack, yet their blood pressure and cholesterol are normal. They do not smoke, they exercise, do not have diabetes, and there is no family history of heart problems. Even so, based upon their complaints of chest pain, the ER docs would be remiss not to do the appropriate testing. Much to their surprise, the tests come back positive for an acute MI, (doctor talk: myocardial infarction). Yes, a heart attack! What is going on? Well, after much research, we now understand that there are other significant risk factors. This chapter is going to look at them:

- *Anger*

- *Negative Attitude*

- *Depression*

- *Elevated C-Reactive Protein (CRP)*

- *Homocysteine Eleation*

Anger

Stating that emotions affect the heart should come as no surprise to anyone. Aside from the metaphorical aspect, suffer a fright and your heart begins to pound. Get angry and your blood pressure goes up. Years ago we became familiar with the term Type-A Personality, those people who were considered to be highly aggressive, and who were more prone to heart attacks. Type-A's were described as hard driving, competitive individuals. It later turned out that the type-A description failed to include "excessive anger and hostility," factors now associated with heart disease.

Historically, we have noted that certain people in the midst of a major argument, fight, or disagreement are prone to have a cardiac incident during or after the battle. We thought that the fight was a triggering mechanism for the attack, not a specific risk factor. Now, numerous studies indicate that those who become irritated at the slightest provocation have a 50% greater chance of a heart attack.

This includes personality traits such as:

- A hot temper.

- Interrupting others in the middle of a sentence.

- Feeling a flush or irritation when they're interrupted.

- A dominating personality (over others) or,

- A high level of irritability.

All of these aggressive traits place the individual at a greater risk of heart problems than others, irrespective of whether or not they have the traditional risk factors. Anger in men usually starts when they are young. Research is now indicating that men in their 20s, who are angry and over reactive to stressful situations, have a five times greater chance of having a heart attack by the time they reach age 50. Women on the other hand, generally do not react as aggressively as men do when they are irritated or angered. Women will show their anger in different, more subtle ways, but the process is basically the same, and in the end results in heart disease. That is not to say women do not have tempers and yell and scream, but the macho personality of many men causes them to react more frequently and more violently than women.

Depression

For many years physicians have considered depression and heart disease as companions, and as such, each could lead to the other. Research now shows us that depression is a very significant risk factor for a heart attack. A study of 1,500 people over a 14-year period found that those who suffered from depression were four times more likely to suffer from heart disease.

A study at Johns Hopkins enrolled 1,190 male medical students between 1948 and 1964 and followed their health status for 40 years. The incidence of depression was found to be 12% among that population. Among that 12% the rate of heart attacks was four times greater than that of their peers.

Depression also seems to be a significant risk factor for high blood pressure. The Centers for Disease Control published the results of a study of 3,000 men who initially had a normal blood pressure. During the 16 years of follow-up, depression was found to triple the risk of developing high blood pressure.

In March of 2001, a study published in the journal *Psychosomatic Medicine* looked at 5,000 members of a labor union sponsored high blood pressure program. All were screened for depression. The results showed that those with a history of depression were twice as likely to have a heart attack to those without that history.

Study after study results in the same conclusions: Depression is a very important risk factor for heart disease. In addition, cardiologists continually report that their depressed patients have a higher degree of mortality after their heart attack, or open-heart surgery.

Inflammation & C-Reactive Protein

I try to keep my patients, as well as my audiences, as up to date as possible. I do this by keeping myself up on the most current medical literature, and by attending as many medical meetings as possible.

The latest, exciting news about the cause of heart disease and plaque deposition has to do with inflammation. Yes, inflammation is the new buzzword at medical meetings.

It all began with the finding that a protein, which in the past was used to measure liver inflammation, was now being found in heart disease. This is called the C-reactive protein or CRP. In the past, if we were concerned that a patient might have viral hepatitis, we would do a series of tests to see if the liver was inflamed. One of these tests was the CRP. Since they monitor inflammatory changes in the tissue, the questions came up, Why are they elevated in heart disease? Is there an inflammatory process going on in the body that is involved in heart disease? Does the whole process of plaque deposition start because of inflammation in the arteries? And if it does, what is causing the inflammation? Cardiologists and other researchers started to get very interested in this phenomenon.

A similar question was raised several years ago when an Australian doctor found signs of inflammation associated with ulcer disease. He claimed his research demonstrated that much too everyone's surprise, ulcers were caused by bacteria. Yes, I said bacteria. *Helicobacter Pylori or H. Pylori.* Most doctors thought of him as a nut case. After all, we all knew that ulcers were caused by stress, alcohol, and smoking. Well, after much more laborious research, including the Australian doctor swallowing this H. Pylori bug and giving himself ulcers, the medical community finally accepted this concept. Today we treat and cure 80% of ulcers with antibiotics.

Getting back to heart disease, the researchers started looking to see if a similar bacterium was involved in heart disease. If it was, this could explain the rise in the CRP. In their search, they started culturing tissue associated with the plaque formation. They took samples of this plaque from patients all over this country, and placed it in petri dishes to see what would grow. Again, much to their surprise, a common bacterium was found. It was not the *H. pylori*, but another one called *Chlamydia pneumonia*.

This started to raise doctors' eyebrows all over the world. Were bacteria the cause of heart disease, just like ulcers? If bacteria were the problem, where were they coming from? Researchers then started looking at potential locations in the body and came up with the gums as the possible source. Dentists who specialized in gum diseases were then surveyed. They questioned their patients and found a significant relationship between those with advanced gum disease and heart disease. For the first time dentists began sending their patients directly to cardiologists. And that's when flossing became the buzz word.

You realize that if all of this proves to be true, we will soon be treating and curing heart disease with antibiotics. Wow!!! That is exciting! How soon before this is a reality, I don't know, but at the rate the research is being done, it may well be in the next couple of years. Stay tuned!

Getting back to anger, attitude, and depression, the question is: How do they do their harm? Here is the current thinking on how all three are related as risk factors for heart disease. Remember I said that the plaque deposits on the wall of the arteries. Because of that, the arteries, with time, actually become so blocked that blood cannot pass in sufficient amounts. We discussed the possibility that a bacteria irritated the lining of the artery and that this irritation caused the inflammation. Well, now the thinking is that plaque deposition is a multistage process that follows this progression:

Irritation → Inflammation → C-Reactive Protein elevation → LDL cholesterol deposition → plaque formation.

The role that anger, attitude and depression plays, is based upon the fight or flight syndrome. You get angry, you have a bad attitude—or you are depressed and you produce a fight or flight reaction with its resultant release of cortisol and adrenalin. These hormones then produce the inflammation, which then stimulates the elevation of the C-reactive protein and the process begins. That would sure solve the mystery of why the CRP is elevated.

Since we have now identified elevated CRPs as a significant risk factor for heart disease, let's identify the ways of decreasing it.

Right on top of the list is the statin drugs. These are the miracle drugs of the new millennium. Not only do they do all of those wonderful things for cholesterol problems, but doctors have now discovered that they will also lower the CRPs and decrease the damage caused by the inflammation. In addition, since emotions can play such a significant role in the release of the cortisol and the associated inflammation, anything that you can do to impact the emotions would be beneficial. So…

- Start working on controlling the road rage and anger

- Stop carrying grudges

- Identify, accept, and deal with depression

- Exercise will be very beneficial

- And lastly, I urge you as strongly as I can, learn and practice MEDITATION!

Homocysteine

This amino acid has recently been shown to play a role as a risk factor for heart disease and stroke. Evidence now shows that homocysteine may cause its damage by irritating the lining of the arteries and promoting blood clots. While absolute evidence is still lacking, enough information is available to suggest that all, and especially those at higher levels of risk, should take the necessary steps to decrease their levels. This is simply done by increasing the intake of vitamin B6 and B12 and folic acid.

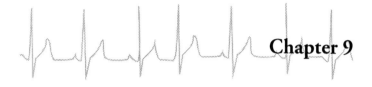

Chapter 9

CHANGE YOUR ATTITUDE—
CHANGE YOUR LIFE

The latest research includes your attitude as a risk factor for heart disease. According to a study at the Johns Hopkins Medical School, a "positive attitude may offer the strongest known protection against heart disease," while a bad attitude may put you "at great risk."

They looked at 600 adults with a family history of heart disease. Those in the study with a "good" attitude were half as likely as their counterparts to experience a heart event such as a heart attack or sudden death. The results were adjusted for all of the traditional risk factors. These exciting conclusions demonstrated that positive thinking and attitude, regardless of age, sex, or race, played a very important role in preventing heart disease.

Well, as we have discussed in previous chapters, your attitude controls every aspect of real life, so it stands to reason that a negative attitude will ultimately have direct impact on your heart. We know that *coping* is the major tool that we use to deal with stressful situations. Unfortunately, many of us do not cope well, and stressful situations start producing medical problems.

It is the inability to cope that directly impacts the release of cortisol and adrenaline into the blood stream. This produces the classic fight or flight reaction. Your blood pressure goes up, your heart rate increases, and the heart gets involved.

So the personality trait that allows you to become angered, irritated, or frustrated is the same personality trait that allows the negative response by the heart. If you have identified yourself as having one of these traits, the question you should rightfully ask is, "So, how do I change?"

I realize that as one increases in years, your personality becomes more difficult to alter or change. But the first step in solving or altering a problem is to accept that you *have* the problem.

Be honest with yourself. For if you lie to yourself, you are ultimately hurting yourself and you will never get to the root of the problem. No one knows better than you do how you react to stressful situations. I know there are all degrees of anger and temper. When I ask a patient, "Do you get angry?" I frequently hear, "Sure, but I can control it." My response to that comment is, "*Your* evaluation of *your* anger is very subjective. Look to your spouse or significant other for a more objective answer."

A good example of anger and the harm it does is the phenomenon we are seeing a great deal of in recent years called road rage. As I travel around the world lecturing to male and female executives, I often ask the question, "How many in the audience have experienced road rage?" The response I get is very interesting. Most men do not raise their hands.

However, I've noticed that if the men's wives are present and the question is asked, when no hands go up I see the wives turning toward their husbands with a pained look on their faces. It's as if they are thinking, "Are you kidding? You yell and scream if someone just *thinks* about cutting you off. One of these days the wind is going to blow your middle finger off!"

Once you have accepted the fact that there is or may be a problem, you can take the appropriate steps to correct it. Things such as spirituality and prayer, anger management clinics, relaxation techniques, exercise, and cognitive therapy all are beneficial. Please do not forget to include meditation and deep breathing. And remember the first step: Accept that you have a problem.

When we look at anger or the inability to cope with daily stressors, I think it is important that we consider and evaluate what it is in our basic makeup that produces these reactions. What causes us to get angry? I don't mean a specific event; I mean what is there in our personality that dictates how we react. What makes us all different? Why do some of us demonstrate road rage, get into arguments and fights, and get illnesses? Do these reactions find their beginnings in our infancy or childhood? Are they present at birth? Is there a genetic component? And of course, the reason for this book, how do these emotions impact our hearts and our longevity?

Fortunately, some very exciting research has recently been done that answers many of these questions. Psychologists have known for years that the human mind has been involved in our behavior and health. But what specifically causes us to do the things we do? Why do we get depressed, anxious, become neurotic, or obsessed? Why do so many of our illnesses have as their basis these conditions?

Freud and his colleagues, past and present, felt that we are victims of our environment.(That the things that happened to us in our early years, come back to haunt us and cause illness.) Psychosomatic illnesses have been suggested as the culprit for decades. It has always been easier to say we have a headache than to admit we have an emotional problem. Identifying what is going on and what we can do about it will certainly help us keep our heart alive longer.

Psychologists have established that one of the basic responses that separate us is our moods, our happiness, and our optimism. They have told us that happy people do not get angry as easily. That optimistic people enjoy good physical health, longer life, and greater happiness. They also tell us that with the use of modern technology, they can measure the brain's response to happiness. How many times have you heard a parent of a newborn brag about their son or daughter as being such a happy child? Now with the use of MRIs and other new electronic devices we can actually measure the brain's activity in the area of mood. Happy children have much more activity in their prefrontal lobe of the brain. They can literally record a higher degree of activity as the child laughs and plays.

Behaviorists also have done research on Tibetan monks in deep meditation.(The greater the degree of calm, the greater the joy, the more positive the response, the more the activity in this same area of the brain.) Based upon this and other responses, researchers now strongly believe that happiness can be inborn, a genetic trait. (That the happy infant is literally born with a higher level of joy.) That those of us who cope, don't get angry as easily, are born with this trait. Psychiatrists now generally accept that depression is caused by a biochemical change in the brain, and that many of these changes are genetically transmitted.

Study after study has shown that happiness and optimism give the body a greater response to illness, and that the immune system, which is responsible for keeping us healthy, is much more active in these individuals. The body responds to these behaviors and produces the cells and antibodies that are needed to avoid infection or cancer. Heart disease and high blood pressure are also found less frequently.

So now that we know about all of these good things, what do those of us do who were not blessed with these good genes? What steps can we take to improve our optimism, to increase our happiness, and to live longer?

Our happiness levels are instilled in our prefrontal area of the brain at birth. They respond just like a thermostat. You set it for a certain level and it always goes back to that level. Can you change the level, that is, can you change the thermostat? Scientists believe you can. You can do things to increase your happiness, your optimism.

The first step is to establish where your thermostat is set. How happy are you?

A test to measure your level of happiness was developed by Edward Diener, a psychologist at the University of Illinois. His test is based upon your answers to the following:

Score your answers on the scale from 1 to 7

1 to 3 = not true at all

3 to 5 = moderately true

5 to 7 = absolutely true

My life is close to ideal in most ways:

     1 2 3 4 5 6 7

The conditions of my life are excellent:

     1 2 3 4 5 6 7

I am satisfied with my life:

     1 2 3 4 5 6 7

So far I have gotten the important things in my life:

     1 2 3 4 5 6 7

If I could live my life over, I would change nothing:

     1 2 3 4 5 6 7

Total your scores.

     31 to 35 = Your life is extremely satisfying

     26 to 30 = You are very satisfied

     21 to 25 = You are slightly satisfied

     15 to 19 = You are slightly dissatisfied

     10 to 14 = You are dissatisfied

Below 10 = You are extremely dissatisfied

If you scored low, what can you do to increase your happiness?

It is very surprising. National surveys about the things that will make you happier are not related to possessions or money, but to...

1. Increasing your relationships: make more friends

2. Become more spiritual

3. Do more to help others

4. Accomplish goals

5. Become more creative

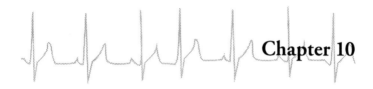

Chapter 10

IT'S ALL ABOUT COPING

No discussion of risk factors involved in heart attacks would be complete without including the role that stress and being able to cope with it plays.

First, what I say next is probably going to surprise you. Contrary to what we've been taught, *I do not consider* stress *to be harmful.* I do not think stress is our enemy. (I'll bet you read that sentence twice.)

Countless books have been written, innumerable lectures have been given, and untold doctor-patient conversations have taken place, all discussing the role of stress on our lives. It has been blamed for almost every calamity and most, if not all, of the illnesses we get.

Here is where I differ:

I think stress is the stimuli we all need to function. It is an integral part of our daily activity. Without it we would not accomplish the things we have. If we were not stressed to take some action, we would probably just sit in our chairs like a blob. Our goals, our drive for success, our achievements would not have been accomplished without the stimuli that stress provides.

In my experience, problems develop when we are stimulated (stressed) and then cannot *cope* with the stress. When we are confronted with a challenge, given a difficult task, or placed in a hostile environment, we react. If we react *negatively* and we fail to *cope* with the event, problems then develop. This is where I believe medical troubles occur.

So to drive home the point, I'm going to repeat myself. The problem is NOT the stresses in our lives. Then what is it? I submit that the health problems occur when we become "dis-stressed" When we are "dis-stressed," our blood pressure goes up, we may develop a skin rash, or have an anxiety attack.

This point is so critical, I feel it bears repeating:

It is not the stress that causes the problem; it is the inability to cope with the stress that produces the dis-stress and illness.

Almost every single day, stressors invade our lives. Most of us deal with them effortlessly. We cope and go on with business as usual. In other words, as long as you are adequately coping with your stressors, doing well and not reacting by getting some illness from them, stress is essentially not harmful.

I like to use the example of two equal business partners Bob and Ted. They are both at an important meeting. Information is presented that has the potential to be very destructive to their company. They both hear the same statements. Bob yells and pounds on the table. "Oh my gosh, I'm ruined!" Tom, however, listens calmly, all the while figuring out a solution, a common-sense plan to deal with the bad news. Obviously the first partner, Bob, is not coping. His blood pressure is going way up as he is panicking. He is a victim of distress. The second partner, Tom, has the ability to cope. He accepts the news (stress), deals with it, and goes on with his life. His health remains normal.

Why one person and not another has difficulty coping is a complicated subject. Genetics, childhood environments with the associated personality development each play a role. All of us react differently to stressful situations. Some yell, argue, throw things, fight, or just get very angry. Suffice it to say, the more we doctors learn about stress, the more we realize how important of a role it plays.

Therefore, learning how to *cope* is vital in trying to decrease your risk of having a heart attack. We all know of people who have had a heart attack soon after a very stressful situation. In addition to the many patients I've seen with a history of a major emotional experience prior to their heart attack, I had a personal experience with a very close family member. He was in business with a partner. His partner was not very ethical and decided he was going to take the business away from my relative. Weeks of arguing and legal battles paid their toll. My relative suffered a near-fatal heart attack in the middle of one of their fights. He ended up losing his business. One year later he was dead from colon cancer.

I'll bet most of you have had, or heard of, similar experiences. Think about the people you know and what preceded their heart problems or other illness. If we could only learn how to cope with those stressors, what a difference it would make in our overall health!

First, let's look at what is going on in our body. What is producing the heart attack? We know that the entire experience of failing to cope with its associated "dis-stress" produces a significant biochemical reaction. Remember the fight or flight reaction? Dr. Hans Seyle at McGill University in Canada, demonstrated that when the body is stimulated to react to a stressful situation, whether it be thoughts, words or acts, a message is sent directly to the adrenal gland. This is the gland responsible for getting us out of a dangerous situation. It does this by releasing a chemical called "catacholamines" (adrenalin and cortisol). These then cause our heart to beat faster and our blood pressure to go up so we can get out of the threatening situation as fast as possible. They also cause us to breathe more rapidly and in many cases to start perspiring.

Those reactions, designed to help us, unfortunately can also harm us. The elevated blood pressure and the effect of the adrenalin on the heart can play a significant role in causing a heart attack. These hormones also can also create an inflammatory reaction in the lining of the arteries, and as we discussed in past chapters, this inflammation is the beginning of clogging of the vessel.

In addition to its impact on the heart, failing to cope also creates a problem in the immune system. Remember, the immune system is responsible for keeping us free from disease--all disease, including cancer. To see what response *failing to cope* has on the immune system, several studies have been done on medical students. The immune system's primary responsibility is to keep our body free from disease. It does this by producing cells that have as their main job finding and destroying the enemy.

The enemy is bacteria, viruses, fungi, and cancer cells. One of the major cells doing this is called the T cell. It swims through our body searching for the enemy cells. When it finds them, it destroys them. The reason AIDS patients get some weird infections is because the HIV virus destroys the T cell, so the body cannot react to the invading disease.

Getting back to the students, scientist were curious as to why they were getting increased infections during their exams. They took blood samples one month prior to finals and did T cell counts. One month later, during the exams they drew another round of blood samples, and did a second T cell count. What they found was very interesting. The blood count prior to finals was normal, the one during finals had a decreased number of these T cells. This demonstrated that during periods of increased stress, those students who had infections were not coping. For the first time, this scientifically demonstrated that coping directly can affect the immune system. These responses are the first of several excellent examples of the mind-body reaction.(A physiologic response, with obvious signs and symptoms, occurring simply because of the inability to cope with stress.)

After all of my experiences with my patients, I am convinced that many of the illness we get are because of the effect of the stressors on the immune system. The medical student research is just one of many examples. Think about your own personal family members or friend's experiences. Try to relate a negative or emotional occurrence prior to the onset of an illness.

I have a concept that I now want to share with you. I have discussed the miracle of our bodies several times. The ways our various systems function on their own. Again, I will say I don't know about creationism versus the big bang theory. What I do know and believe is that some power or force created this edifice we call our body. It gave us all of the systems we need to survive. I have difficulty understanding how such a fantastic creation would have evolved without a method of keeping it free from disease. Based upon the fact that it has taken us thousands of years to develop the left side (logic and thought) of our brain, and that we are just starting to understand and develop the right side of the brain (intuition and creativity). I believe that hidden in the right side is the ability to control and prevent many of the illness we get.

The whole mind-body response to me is just the beginning of our understanding of the potential to self-heal. The effect on healing and longevity that a positive attitude has been to me is very significant. We are at the tip of the iceberg in understanding these potentials. How long it will take I do not know, but I am confidant that some day we will develop them.

Now a question based on logic: "If your mind can stimulate a harmful or negative response, why can it not do the opposite and stimulate a beneficial or positive effect?" This is the basis of the whole discussion of the mind-body reaction and the immune system.

Back to stress and "dis-stress." As I mentioned, it is only when you cannot cope with your stress that you get ill and it becomes dis-stress. So the obvious question is, How can I learn to cope, or what can I do so that I can change?

There are many tools available to all of us in dealing with coping. biofeedback, meditation, yoga, exercise and relaxation skills all work to varying degrees, depending on the individual. A little dedication and motivation is needed.

Drugs can also help combat distress. I generally do not recommend them because of their habit forming, dependency problems. But for acute problems, and only when prescribed by your physician, certain ones will work.

Any of the above methods can do the job. Since I like to keep things as simple as possible, I suggest learning the skills of relaxation and meditation. They are easy to practice; no special equipment is needed and they can be done almost anywhere. What you need is a quiet environment and a comfortable chair. The technique is based on letting your mind relax by concentrating on limited thoughts. This concept is suggested in the book *The Relaxation Response* by Herbert Benson M.D., (Avon Books), and I strongly suggest reading it.

The most difficult part of relaxing the brain is to stop it from thinking. The brain never rests; even in sleep it is active. The whole concept of meditation is built on the principle of letting the mind get some well deserved rest. Why we in Western cultures have never fervently adopted this lifesaving procedure amazes me. Eastern cultures have for centuries practiced meditation as a healing and calming tool. I say it is time we began teaching this in our medical and other healing schools.

If you are not currently doing so, I strongly suggest that you get up, step out of your comfort zone, put aside your conservative thinking, and for the benefit of your loved ones, open yourself up to the experience and the benefits of so-called New Age practices. Don't just dismiss yoga, meditation, or relaxation techniques because you think you're too old to learn new tricks. If you truly want to live longer and enjoy life with your family and friends...

PUT DOWN THAT REMOTE! GET OUT OF THAT LA-Z-BOY!

TAKE ACTION!

TREAT YOUR HEART RIGHT, AND IT WILL TREAT YOU RIGHT!

To follow is a basic meditation technique that will help you to relax:

- Find a comfortable place to sit.

- Get comfortable in your chair or seat.

- Place your hands on your lap.

- Close your eyes.

- Start concentrating on your breathing.

- Listen to the sounds your breathing makes.

- Other thoughts will come into your mind, but let them go.

- Just think about your breathing.

- Identify a series of simple, comforting words, words that you would say in a religious environment, or words that you would say to a loved one.

- As you breathe out, repeat the words.

- Continue this for 20 minutes.

When you find yourself in a difficult situation, I strongly urge a few moments of meditation. Twenty minutes is best, but just as with exercise, *any is better than none.*

In addition to learning meditation on your own, there are many tapes available that will assist. The Mind/Body Medical Institute at Harvard has several that I would recommend and they can be reached on their Web site, mbmi.org.

Additionally, let me also suggest that putting things in perspective can also be very beneficial. When something happens that upsets you, stop and ask yourself, "Will this be important a year from now?" Or, "What will I accomplish by getting upset?" This technique may sound overly simple, but what do you have to lose by trying it? I have seen it produce amazing results for several of my patients who walked into my office as big-time skeptics.

10 Steps For Coping

1. Find time daily to meditate.

2. Don't feel like you have to do *everything.*

3. Accept that you have limitations.

4. Develop a support network.

5. Smile and laugh more.

6. Show kindness, pick up liter, open doors for others.

7. Become more spiritual.

8. Get more exercise.

9. Avoid negative people.

10. Maintain a positive attitude.

REMEMBER YOU HAVE THE POWER...

YOUR ATTITUDE CONTROLS YOUR DESTINY!

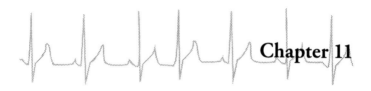

Chapter 11

HOW IMPORTANT
ARE VITAMINS?

Should You Take Them?

If I had to rate questions as to their frequency, this one would be way up on the top of the list, along with the effectiveness of the Atkins diet. I always start off the answer with the following disclaimer:

"My answer now is far different than it was 10 years ago."

I will admit that when I graduated from medical school, and during the first 25 years of my practice, my answer to that question was right out of the mouths of my professors: "There is no need for anyone who eats a balanced diet to supplement it with those phony pills. What you are accomplishing is putting money in the pockets of those snake-oil salesmen. Your body has no need for them."

Well, that was what I used to say. Yes I am a convert! I think back to those days in medical school and I reflect on our education on the subject of nutrition. We did not get any!

We learned about vitamins and minerals in our biochemistry class. Fortunately, today that is all changing. Nutrition and mind-body are becoming an integral part of medical education.

(Back to vitamins.) Based upon my comments in previous chapters, and valid data to support their use, I am a strong advocate of certain vitamins, especially the ones with increased antioxidants. So vitamin C and vitamin E are high on my list. I also recommend the use of folic acid and the B complex vitamins.

In discussing vitamins, it is important to mention that all vitamins are not without risk. We divide them into two groups: fat-soluble and water-soluble.

Water-Soluble

- Vitamin C and the B complex
- Niacin

Fat-Soluble

- Vitamin E, D, and A

When water-soluble vitamins are taken in large doses, (except for niacin) the body absorbs what it needs and excretes the rest as waste. Have you ever noticed the bright yellow color of your urine after taking a large dose of B complex?

On the other hand, large doses of fat-soluble vitamins can stay in the body and can cause problems. Because of that, you do not want to exceed 25,000 units of vitamin

A, 800 IU's (international units) of vitamin E and 400 IU's of vitamin D per day. There is a condition called hypervitaminosis where too much of vitamins A, E or D can cause problems such as jaundice, and toxicities associated with vitamin D metabolism. Too much vitamin E can result in greater incidences of chronic diseases.

I will never forget my first experience with hypervitaminosis A. I was a senior medical student on rotation in the ER of the county hospital. It was a typical, busy day when the paramedics brought in, by ambulance, a homeless-looking gentleman. Since this was the county hospital the majority of our patients either were alcoholics, homeless, or drug addicts. I was assigned to do the H & P (history and physical). Most senior medical students, especially if it is close to graduation, are rather cocky. Yes we had an attitude. We were the best, and any patient coming to our hospital was going to get the best care, not like what happens in the outside PMD environment (private medical doctor).

I examined the patient and the first thing I noticed, he was very jaundiced (yellow). Well, with practically every patient being an alcoholic, and since most alcoholics have cirrhosis of the liver, and since cirrhosis causes jaundice, the obvious diagnosis was "ADD" (another dammed drunk). Doctors love initial abbreviations.

When I was done with my exam, I went to the resident in charge to tell him what I had. My diagnosis was alcoholic cirrhosis with jaundice.

I ordered the appropriate lab work. It came back and much to my surprise his liver profile was okay. (The resident saw the results and immediately ordered a serum for vitamin A. Lo and behold, it was very high). This gentleman had hypervitaminosis A. I lost a little of my cockiness that day. I did not get a complete history, so I did not find out until later that in a drunken stupor, this patient went looking for food in a trashcan behind a drug store. And he came upon discarded, outdated vitamin A pills. He thought they were candy and swallowed most of them. The elevated level of vitamin A caused his skin to turn yellow. I was very embarrassed by missing that diagnosis, but I sure learned about the know-it-all attitude.

In summary, my suggestion on the use of vitamins and minerals is that they are beneficial, and I have no problem with their (limited) use. If you choose to take them, make sure that the dosages are effective and safe (see my Daily Game Plan in the tear-out section). And restrict your intake of the fat-soluble ones.

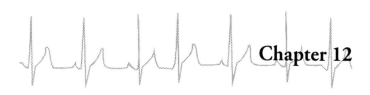

Chapter 12

THE ROLE OF ANTIOXIDANTS

If you would have suggested five years ago that I would be strongly recommending that everybody should take antioxidants, or that at meetings of the prestigious American Heart Association, world- renowned cardiologists would be urging their use, I would have told you that you're crazy. I'd have laughed and said, "That's the stuff 'health nuts' hype and sell to make a fortune." Well it looks like I am about to eat a little crow. Antioxidants are now not only widely recognized, but highly recommended at medical meetings all over the world. Based upon that, I would be remiss if I did not include a chapter on what they are, and why doctors now suggest their daily intake for everyone.

First, what are Antioxidants?

To understand their role we first have to understand that every cell in our body is part of a gigantic electrical system. All electricity is based upon two components called ions.(A positively charged one and a negatively charged one.) These two together provide the balance that allows the cells to function. Every cell in our body has these positive and negative charges. Chemists refer to them as radicals. In addition, coming into every cell as we breath is the basic chemical we need to survive: oxygen. When the oxygen enters the cell it creates a problem for the nicely balanced negative and positive radicals. One of them is going to have to leave to make room for the intruder, oxygen, since the cell balance is dependent on two balancing radicals. The radical that leaves goes out into the circulation looking for a new home or cell. This homeless electrical charge is now known as a free radical. Now, here is where the antioxidant comes into play. When this free radical enters its new home, it creates a problem. This problem is called oxidation. Researchers now think that this oxidative process is the beginning of aging, and may very well be the start of heart disease and cancer.

Obviously, the damage the free radical causes is more complicated, but for the sake of this explanation, let's just say that when this free radical enters the cell, it interferes with the normal cell behavior, and abnormal processes start. In order to prevent this damage, the body produces something called antioxidants. Their role is to prevent oxidation and its resultant damage to the cell. The more antioxidants you can produce or have available, the better off you are.

Doctors are finally starting to realize how important the antioxidants are in preventing disease. We also understand that as people age, our ability to produce antioxidants decreases. Because of that, their intake is now strongly recommended.

So where do we get the antioxidants? Certain foods:

Cooked Tomatoes (Lycopene)

This is what gives the tomato the red color.

Researchers at the Harvard School of Public Health studied the eating habits of 47,000 men over six years. Information coming out of that study demonstrated that men who consumed a diet high in cooked tomatoes (at least 10 servings per week) had a significant decrease in the risk of heart disease and prostate cancer when compared to men who did not. The lycopene is present in all tomatoes, but apparently the cooking process frees up more of it.

Blueberries

Research done at the USDA nutrition center found that blueberries rank # 1 in antioxidant activity when compared to 40 other fresh fruits and vegetables. The pigment that makes the blueberry blue is thought to be responsible for this major health benefit.

Tea

For several years, scientists have suggested that daily tea drinking may be associated with improved health. Finally research is documenting the role that tea plays. Most of the studies have been done using green or black tea, but now a tea that dates back to the Ming Dynasties is getting some notoriety. Have you have heard of white tea? This is a tea that is primarily found in China's Fujian province. Traditionally black and white tea are processed by taking fresh leaves and drying or withering them before being crushed, then steamed or fermented. With white tea, the leaves are immediately steamed, then dried. This leaves much more of their basic chemistry intact. As a result of this, the white tea has a much higher amount of polyphenols. These are very potent antioxidants and are reported to be very effective in promoting dental health and in cancer prevention. The only reported negative is that because of the different processing methods they seem to have a higher caffeine stimulant effect.

A paper presented at the 50th annual meeting of the American College of Cardiology reported that in a combined study, those who drank three or more cups of black tea per day had a significant decrease in heart disease when compared to others in the study who did not drink tea.

In addition, studies done in Japan and reported in a recent issue of the American Journal of Cardiology, showed that people who drink a cup of green tea every day may be protecting themselves against a heart attack because the flavonoids, which are abundant in green tea, are very potent antioxidants.

And finally, in the May 2002 issue of *Circulation,* a report indicated that tea consumption is associated with an increased rate of survival following a heart attack.

The conclusion of all of these reports is that the flavonoids have the ability to prevent the LDLs (the bad guys) from doing their damage as well as overall cell protection.

Nuts

This is sort of personal for me because I love nuts and for years I did not eat them because I was concerned about the fat content. Well that is all changing.

My first information on the benefit of nuts came while I was attending a medical meeting a few years ago in Los Angeles. A paper was being presented on the health value of nuts. I went to the talk and was thrilled by what I heard. I was so excited that when the talk was over, I went up to the doctor who presented the information him to thank him for the great news. During our brief conversation I asked him if *all* nuts were included in his study. He answered yes.

I then asked, "Well how about my very favorite nut, the one you get in Hawaii, macadamia nuts?" Again he answered in the affirmative. "They do have a very high-fat content," he added, "so you don't want to eat too many of them." I started to walk away, when another thought came to my mind, I went back and asked, "Okay, how about my all time favorite?" He asked, "What is that?"

"Chocolate covered macadamia nuts!" He looked at me, smiled, and shook his head, "No!" Oh well, I tried.

Question: Just how healthy are nuts?

Answer: Researchers at the Brigham and Women's Hospital in their nationwide "Nurses' Health Study," reported in the British Medical Journal that 86,000 women's eating habits were followed over a 14-year period. Researchers found that the women who ate the most nuts, more than half a cup per week, were about 35% less likely to develop heart disease or suffer a heart attack, than women who rarely or never ate nuts. Another study, done by Dr. Frank

Hu at Harvard, demonstrated that eating one ounce of nuts daily can reduce the risk of heart disease by 30%.

Furthermore, the relationship between nut consumption and heart disease held true even after controlling for differences in exercise, smoking, body weight, and fiber or vitamin intake.

Likewise, in a survey of doctors, called the "Physicians' Health Study," reported at the 71st Annual American Heart Associations Conference in Dallas, 22,000 men were observed over a period of 11 years. Those men whose diets included the most nuts had the lowest risk of dying from heart disease during the study. Again, researchers took care to look at nut consumption independent of other factors like exercise, high blood pressure, smoking, and diabetes.

Question: **So why are nuts so healthy?**

Answer: Nuts are a powerhouse of good nutrition.

- They are loaded with fiber

- Mono and polyunsaturated fats (the good guys)

- Vitamin E

- Folic acid

- Antioxidants

- And they also lower cholesterol

In addition to that, they have been shown to help lower the LDL (remember, the bad guy) and raise the HDL cholesterol (the good guy). Another benefit is in dieting. Studies are now showing that those who snack on nuts tend to weigh less then those who do not.

This is very important, be sure to include at least 1-3 ounces in your daily diet. Walnuts, pecans, and almonds are the best ones. But walnuts win the BEST title because of their high content of omega-3s, (similar to salmon). However, I suggest you eat them only raw or dry roasted.

Red Wine

At a recent meeting of the American Heart Association, a talk entitled "The French Paradox" was presented. For several years we have heard about the fact that the French, who have this horrible, saturated fat diet with all that butter, cream, cheese, and fatty meats, still have a lower incidence of heart disease than we have. The question that needed to be answered was, WHY?

First of all, even though they do eat a lot of saturated fats, the volume of food they take in is half of what we consume. When you have a meal served to you in France, the plate is half full. In the U.S., the food is falling off of the sides.

On top of that, they consume a large quantity of red wine.

It turns out that the red grape skin that is fermented to make the wine has a very high content of an antioxidant called reveratrol. And it's this intake of the red wine that is keeping their arteries healthy. The good news for those who, for whatever reason, do not want to drink wine, you can get the same benefits from red grape juice.

When the professor who gave the paper was asked what he personally drinks, he answered, "When I get up in the morning, I have grape juice instead of orange juice, and at dinner I have red wine."

Fish

I will repeat my ever-so-important recommendation. EAT FISH AND GET THOSE POWERFUL OMEGA-3s. They are a great source of antioxidants. Remember, salmon, shellfish, trout, and herring (all fatty fish) are the best. For those who do not like or eat fish, the fish oil capsules are a good substitute for the omega 3s.

Cocoa

New studies indicate that cocoa is an excellent source of antioxidants. When you eat chocolate (dark only), it is still good, except you are adding calories.

And finally, soy products, pomegranate juice, and flax seeds are also good sources of antioxidants.

In summary, study after study have shown that increased antioxidants in the diet have had a significant impact on decreasing heart disease.

SO TAKE THEM!

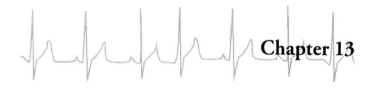

Chapter 13

ASPIRIN, THE MIRACLE DRUG

I now want to spend some time discussing the miracle drug aspirin and its benefit in heart disease.

I call it a miracle drug because it seems like every year a new use is reported. For decades it has been used as a pain reliever and body-temperature reducer. I don't think there is a person reading this book who has not taken an aspirin at some point in their lives. It also was used for many years as the best treatment for arthritis because of its anti-inflammatory properties. Researchers say that if aspirin had to go before the FDA for approval today, it probably would not pass because its exact method of working is still not understood.

Most recently another use was discovered. If you have had a colonoscopy and were told that you have colonic polyps, which are the precursors of colon cancer, you might be interested to know that aspirin has been reported to inhibit their formation.

But let's look at the role they play in heart disease. The current recommendation is that all adults, who do not have any reason not to take them, (allergy, ulcer disease, or conflicting medications), take one *81 mg., enteric coated* aspirin a day. These used to be on the market as baby aspirin. But due to the incidence of Reyes syndrome in infants, they were removed from the market. They are now back on the market specifically for prevention of heart attack and stroke. The reason they are enteric coated is that aspirin can be an irritant to the stomach. By coating them, they are dissolved and absorbed lower down in the intestine.

When I ask audiences, "Why do you think we recommend aspirin?" the usual answer I get is, "It thins the blood." In reality, aspirin does a little more than that.

To understand its role we must first talk about a group of cells, similar to the red cells circulating in our bodies, called platelets. Here is another example of the miracle of our bodies. These platelets have a specific function. Each one of them has a sticky, glue-like material on their surface. These cells are the basic cell involved in the formation of a clot. You'll remember, if you took a Red Cross first-aid class, you were told to put direct pressure on a cut so a clot would form and the bleeding would stop. Well, the clot is made up of thousands of platelets. The direct pressure causes the flow of platelets to slow down and the sticky material on their surface causes them to adhere to each other until a clot is formed.

In reality, aspirin does not cause thinning of the blood, but it interferes with the ability of this sticky material to form a clot.

Why is that important in heart problems? If you recall, earlier I mentioned the formation of plaque in the arteries, and explained how this plaque narrows the openings, hence causing a decrease in the flow of blood.

To understand what happens, I must throw in a little physics. There is a basic principal of physics called "Eddy Currents." This says that, "the smaller the opening, the slower the flow." If we apply this principle to blood flowing through an artery, we understand that as the vessel lumen (or opening) narrows, the velocity of the blood flow decreases. Going back to the direct pressure concept, when the flow slows, the sticky material on the surface of the platelets comes in longer contact and the blood clot forms. Doctors call this clot in the coronary artery a *coronary thrombosis*. This is the basic cause of a heart attack.

So what has this to do with aspirin?

We take aspirin because this miracle pill has the ability to decrease the adhesiveness of the sticky material. Thus, aspirin decreases the ability of a clot to form. Because of that you may bleed longer if you take aspirin on a regular basis because it may take longer for a clot to form, but you *will* clot. Those of you who were told to stop taking aspirin before you had a dental or surgical procedure now understand why.

What I have just described is the prophylactic or preventative use of aspirin. Let's now discuss its therapeutic use. If, by some chance, you've experienced chest pain and went to your local emergency room, the chances are very good the first thing they did was give you an aspirin. This time they used the full strength, 325 mg. aspirin and not the enteric coated. The reason for that is based upon the principles described above. The use of aspirin at the first sign of a heart attack can be life saving. If you start to get chest pain, the clot may already have formed; what the aspirin does is prevent the clot from enlarging. The larger the clot, the more heart muscle is involved, and the greater the chance of extensive damage.

We now recommend that all adults carry with them at all times one full, non coated aspirin (325 mg.). At the first sign of chest pain, take it. If it turns out that the chest pain was not a heart attack, but just some stomach gas, as long as you have no problem (side effects) with aspirin, big deal—you took an aspirin. The potential benefit far outweighs the risk. Taking that aspirin can literally save your life.

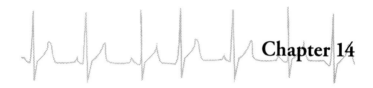

Chapter 14

PLEASURABLE
LIFESTYLE CHANGES

N ow that I have gotten all the heavy stuff out of the way, let me now report on some of the *pleasurable lifestyle changes* that can decrease the incidence of heart disease. Who would have guessed that some of the steps to preventing a fatal disease could be fun?

All of these methods are based upon population surveys as reported in the medical literature. Researchers polled populations around the country and asked them about their habits and medical history.

1. Napping

People who reported taking daily naps had a 50% decrease in heart problems as compared to those who did not nap. More and more information is appearing about the role that sleep deprivation has on our health.

2. Pet Owners

People who own dogs, cats, or other pets had one-fifth of the coronary events. This is because interaction with a pet has a very relaxing effect on the human nervous system.

3. Alcohol

As stated previously, one ounce per day of spirits is associated with a 40% reduction in cardiac events.

4. Sex

In a major study reported in the British Medical Journal, those who participated in more frequent sexual activity had half of all causes of death (mortality) as those who did not.

Based on the above the daily secrets of a long life, you should…

- Take a nap

- Play with your pet

- Have a drink, and

- Then have sex!!!

HOW SWEET IS THAT?

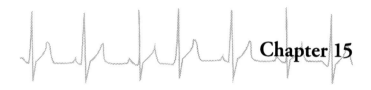

Chapter 15

IS HEART DISEASE
REVERSIBLE?

N ow comes the most important question, If you have been diagnosed with plaque deposits in the walls of your arteries, is there anything you can do about it? In other words is it reversible? If it is not, you have just spent a lot of time learning about something you can do nothing about.

Well the good news is, *the process is reversible!*

A study done by Dr. David Blankenhorn and others called the Monitored Atherosclerosis Regression Study (MARS) done in 1993, had as its objective to establish the effectiveness of a program using a lipid (fat) lowering agent and a diet on a group of patients with significant findings of coronary artery disease.

What he did was to study a group of 270 patients with elevated cholesterol and/or coronary artery disease proven by angiogram. This involves inserting a catheter into to an artery in the groin, injecting a dye into the catheter and following the dye up to the arteries, then taking movies of the dye in the heart arteries and looking for the narrowing where the plaque is deposited.

He then divided the patients into two groups. One group (the test group) was placed on a cholesterol-lowering statin drug (Lovastatin) and a low-cholesterol diet. The other group (the control group) was placed on a placebo (sugar pill). What he found, after several years, was that the group that was on the statin pill (Lovastatin) and diet had a significant regression of the plaque and a slower rate of progression, when compared to the control group.

In other words, *YOU CAN REVERSE THE PROCESS!*

This was the first controlled study to demonstrate this. It's a very significant body of work because it strongly supports the concept of simply dealing with your risk factors to stop the progression of the disease.

What a great piece of research! It is one of my greatest hopes that this information will make *all* of you realize that you can do something about heart disease. Do not take on an attitude that, "It's too late, I already have the disease, and I can't do anything about it." That is absolute nonsense! Consider how fortunate you are to be alive when this miracle group of medications, called STATIN drugs, were developed. There is no question in my mind about how important the statins are in reversing the process. They are vital! I believe strongly that in the not-to-distant future, all adults will be taking these miracle medications on a daily basis, just like they take their vitamins. Even though they may not admit it publicly, many doctors, when surveyed, responded that they are taking a statin, even though they have no heart disease.

Without a doubt, the statin drugs are going to be as important in eliminating heart disease as penicillin was in eliminating bacterial infections.

And finally, another very important study reported by Dr. Dean Ornish at UCSF demonstrated that a very intensive lifestyle change including diet, exercise, meditation, and other relaxing techniques had a significant reduction in angina (chest pain) and the need for open-heart surgery.

You can change the odds; you can control your destiny!

You Can Live to 100 if You Start Taking Corrective Action NOW!

It's in your hands.   Furthermore…

You Can Reverse What You Have Caused!

Yes, You Can Have a Second Chance!

You Can Live to 100 if you start taking corrective action NOW!

It is all up to you!

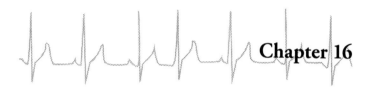

Chapter 16

A LOOK INTO THE FUTURE

We are living in a very exciting time in medicine. The next 25 years are going to be mind boggling when it comes to advances. This is especially going to be true as it relates to heart disease.

Fast forward to the year 2010. Can you imagine a world in which heart disease does not exist? A world free of heart attacks, where you can eat a cheeseburger and not be concerned about the fat content? We are on the verge of that possibility.

The cures of the future most likely will be complex. They will combine genetic, medical, and lifestyle changes. Make the choice, adjust your lifestyle, and you can be around for these fantastic new developments!

Keeping your heart alive for 100 years is going to become much easier with these and other soon-to-come advances:

- A visit to your doctor's office with no more blood tests. The doctor swipes a swab across your inner cheek. From this, all testing is done, including genetic testing. If heart disease looms, your doctor advises a vaccination.

- Prescriptions will be written specifically for you based on your genetic makeup. No longer will you be trying out multiple drugs or dosages. New delivery systems will allow drugs to target specific cells, without damaging other cells. Harmless viruses and bacteria are being identified, and because of their ability to get into a cell, they are going to be used to get the medication to the patient.

- Remember, you want your HDL (the good guy) to be as high as possible because of its ability to get rid of the plaque in the arteries? Well, a new synthetic HDL is being developed that when injected into your arteries, can shrink and eliminate the fat-laden plaque in five weeks.

- This is fantastic! A new medication called "The Poly-Pill" is in the marketing stages in Europe. Remember I told you how great the statin drugs are? This "Poly Pill" will contain all of the ingredients necessary to prevent the deposition of the plaque in the artery and hence decrease heart disease. It will contain a "statin," aspirin, antioxidants, beta-blockers and other necessary drugs all in one, easy-to-swallow capsule. (That's a stock I should buy!)

- As we discussed, cholesterol comes into your body through two ways, your liver makes it, or you eat it. Diet and medication are the two ways we now recommend to decrease the levels. The liver's ability to produce cholesterol differs in all of us, and that difference is often controlled by our genes. Those who are lucky enough to have good genes can eat whatever they want and their cholesterol level does not elevate. For those of us who do not have those good genes, a vaccine is being developed that will stimulate the immune system to block the production of a protein that is involved in cholesterol production, and hence a lower cholesterol.

- In a previous chapter, I have described the heart as a pump. When that pump becomes inefficient because the heart muscle does not do its job due to the effects of increased, chronic, elevated blood pressure, the pump fails. Doctors call that congestive heart failure. Since the pump cannot get the fluid (blood) out into circulation, the fluid backs up in the heart and the chambers become congested. This then causes the muscle to expand and the heart enlarges. It is now an inefficient pump and the legs and lungs and liver fill up with fluid. Obviously this condition has potential serious consequences.

Here comes the good news. To overcome this, and to make the heart a better pump, scientists are now working on taking stem cells from other muscles in the body and injecting them into the heart to grow new heart muscle.

There's another fantastic development for preventing the type of heart failure where the heart enlarges, the muscles become incompetent, and it is no longer an efficient pump. Scientists have now developed a full mesh jacket that is stitched in place around the heart. The jacket envelops the heart preventing it from growing larger, and helping it to maintain its pumping function.

- Another exciting development has to do with those plaque-filled arteries--the ones that get blocked and the blood cannot get through. Well, when these arteries in the heart become totally blocked with plaque, instead of doing bypass surgery, surgeons will simply take stem cells from bone marrow, inject them into the heart, and grow new arteries to replace the clogged ones.

- Defibrillators, the machines that shock the heart back to life, will be as common as fire extinguishers. Every home will have one. They will be voice-activated and will advise you on every step of use, so that defibrillating a stopped heart will be as easy and foolproof as using your TV remote control.

As if that isn't enough, let's look at the advances in heart surgery:

- Minimally invasive open-heart surgery.

Traditional bypass surgery requires opening the chest, exposing the heart and then stopping it from beating. The heart is then hooked up to a heart-lung machine. This does the work of the heart; it oxygenates the blood and then pumps it around the body to all of the vital organs.

The reason the heart is stopped is to allow the surgeons to work on a stationary target, instead of a moving one.

That is all changing. With the new surgical technique called "minimally invasive open-heart surgery," the chest is not opened and the heart is not stopped. A small incision is made in between the ribs. The heart is exposed, and the bypass surgery is performed. These surgeons are so well-trained, they can now work on a moving heart.

Another new technique called "TMR", (transmyocardial revascularization) is being developed. Here, the surgeon uses a laser to punch small holes in the heart muscle. Cardiologists believe that TMR will improve the blood flow to the heart muscle and that will promote new blood vessels to grow, replacing the ones that are clogged with plaque.

- Space Age Surgery

Computers and Star Wars-type robots are finding their way into the operating room. Future surgeons will be developing their skills on computers instead of patients. With the development of three-dimensional MRI, the young surgeons will hone their skills on virtual MRIs of the patient about to have the surgery. Once the techniques are perfected, they will be downloaded into a chip. That chip will then be placed in a robot, which will perform the actual surgery. And, the patient does not have to be in the same city or country as the surgeon. In this new field of neurosurgery, microchips with the entire surgical procedure that has been rehearsed previously, are built into a robotic virtual hand. This hand, situated in the exact proper location, then does the surgery. No hand tremors, no errors because the entire surgery was done previously on a 360-degree rotating model of the patient's anatomy.

In previous chapters we discussed the fact that the heart has several valves to control the flow of blood from one chamber to another. In the past, if these valves became diseased or incompetent, they were replaced by an open-chest procedure. Now, the newest way to replace these bad valves does not require any surgery. A catheter with a synthetic valve, tightly rolled up in it, is threaded under direct visualization up into the area of the valve. The catheter is removed, the rolled up valve is released, it unrolls, and you have a new valve. Wow!

There are new techniques for visualizing the heart and the arteries. A new form of ultra-sound has been developed that can actually look into an artery (IVUS) to see how much plaque there is, and then see how well certain drugs are working.

And finally, a new CAT scanner (CT scanner) has been developed that can look inside the artery walls to evaluate the degree of calcium deposition on the plaque. It gives a read-out, in percentages, of exactly how far the buildup has progressed.

I'm telling you, change your lifestyle so you can enjoy these developments! This is just the beginning!!!

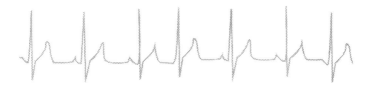

Summary

We have come to the end of the book. What did you learn? No, I am not going to give you a test. The most important thing to remember is *you can control your longevity*. You are in control of your destiny.

I hope you now have embraced the concept that living to 100 is very possible and doable for you.

- Take proper care of your heart and it will take care of you.

- It's easier than you think! Just a few lifestyle changes can make it happen.

- Exercise as often as you can.

- Design the right diet for yourself that is low in saturated fats and high in antioxidants.

- A positive attitude combined with meditation is key to a long life.

- I cannot overemphasize the role that happiness and being optimistic plays.

- Laugh, smile, join many social groups, and most important, control your anger.

- Don't carry grudges. Learn to let them go. They harm you much more that the person you're angry with.

And don't forget the FISH and NUTS!

It's all up to you. You don't have to have heart disease!

I have spent the last five years of my long professional career traveling the world and getting this message out to as many people as I can.

My goal is to get as many hearts as I can to the ripe, *young* age of 100.

Will your heart be a 100-year heart? You owe it to yourself and your loved ones to shout a resounding YES!

About The Author

Dr. Jerry Kornfeld is internationally recognized for his honest and direct discussion of health and medical topics from the mind-body reaction and spirituality, to wellness and coping with stress.

Dr. Jerry has practiced family medicine in Southern California for more than 35 years. He received his Bachelor of Science degree from the University of California, Los Angeles, his medical degree from the University of California, Irvine and did his postgraduate training at the University of Southern California. He then went on to open a private practice specializing in family medicine. From 1988 to 1991 he also served as chief of the Department of Family Practice, Northridge Medial Center in Northridge, California.

From 1993 to 1995, Dr. Jerry served as Medical Director of the Southern California Independent Practice Association, supervising medical quality and health care management issues for more than 60,000 lives. He also served on the Executive Committee of the Quality Improvement Council for the national health plan, Uni-Health America, and he was a member of the Medical Directors Committee for the National IPA Coalition (NIPAC), the organization that develops standards and protocols for California's IPAs (independent practice associations).

In the early 80s, while maintaining his practice, Dr. Jerry launched a public career as an advocate for medical consumers. He broke new ground as the first medical reporter on the ABC affiliate in Los Angeles where he made frequent appearances on *Eyewitness News.* He also served as the on-air medical expert for *AM Los Angeles,* a morning show hosted by Regis Philbin. Recently, he performed a similar service on the nationally syndicated TV show, *Body By Jake.*

Always a relentless researcher of the most up-to-date medical information available, Dr. Jerry came to realize that many of the diseases he was diagnosing were self-induced. Indeed, he was eventually to find out that the number one killer of us all, heart disease, could be prevented and yes, even *reversed.* This realization was the impetus for his most recent book, *Your 100-Year Heart.*

Dr. Jerry remains active as a member of the faculty of UCLA Medical School, teaching freshman students the art of communicating with patients.

He is also in high demand as a motivational speaker specializing in health care issues—especially the critical role of thoughts and attitude on increasing longevity. He travels the world and across the U.S. addressing corporate audiences at multinational companies including Bristol-Meyers Squibb, G.D. Searle and Wyeth Ayerst Laboratories, Copps Food Market and an array of company retreats. Dr. Jerry also addresses medical staffs at hospitals on dealing with depression related to managed care, changes in health care delivery, and the need for doctors to remain committed to their medical oaths. He is also actively involved with Vistage, a global organization of CEOs. The demand for his lectures became so great that he was forced to close his office last year. He also addresses general audiences, sometimes aboard cruise ships, about the things they must do to protect their most important asset, their health.

Dr. Jerry is a prolific writer and contributor to medical and trade publications including recent articles in *Medical Economics, Sharing Ideas* and *Hospital Practice.* He is also author of *Fatherhood Formula*, a resource book for new fathers. Dr. Jerry is a charter diplomate of the American Board of Family Practice and a Charter Fellow of the American Academy of Family Physicians. He is a recipient of a Physician's Recognition Award from the American Medical Association.

Dr. Jerry is very happily married with two successful daughters and two beautiful grandchildren. When not teaching, lecturing, or researching the latest breakthroughs in medicine, his time is spent in his creative passion of black and white art photography. His photos have been published and have appeared in numerous galleries. He is most proud of his recent one-man show at the Las Vegas Museum of Art.

LEARN YOUR RISK FACTORS FOR HEART DISEASE!

Take the following test to learn your risk level.

1 Do you have high blood pressure?

If yes, score 3 points ___

2. Do you have diabetes?

If yes, score 3 points ___

3. Do you smoke?

If yes, score 3 points ___

4. Is your Cholesterol/ HDL ratio 6 or above?

If yes, score 3 points ___

5. Has one or both parents had a heart attack before age 60?

If yes, score 3 points ___

6. Do you get very little exercise?

If yes, score 3 points ___

7. Are you obese?

If yes, score 2 points ___

8. Do you cope with stress poorly?

9. Are you "hot tempered"?

10. Are you sad frequently?

Add up your scores: _____

If your total score is between 20 and 26, you are a heart attack waiting to happen! And obviously the more points you score, the greater your statistical risk of a heart attack. But that does not mean you should put your head in the ground like an ostrich and wait for the event. The whole purpose of this book is to help you identify your risks, then take action and deal with them. Start your "action plan" now!!

Follow the steps outlined.

YOU GET TO MAKE THE CHOICE!

15 EASY STEPS TO PREVENT & REVERSE HEART DISEASE

1. Exercise (any is better than none)

2. Fish, Omega-3s (fish oil) 4-5 times/week

3. 81 mg., enteric coated aspirin daily

4. Antioxidants (Vitamins C and E)

5. Statin drugs (by prescription only)

6. Smile and laugh more

7. Red wine or grape juice

8. Nuts (especially almonds, pecans, walnuts)

9. Cooked tomatoes

10. All teas

11. Decrease saturated and trans fats in your diet

12. Practice meditation

13. Deal with depression (and do not hold grudges)

14. Maintain positive thoughts and attitude

15. Avoid negative people and surroundings

TAKE CARE OF YOUR HEART & IT WILL TAKE CARE OF YOU!

THINGS THAT GIVE OUR HEART PROBLEMS

1. The foods we eat

2. Smoking

3. Sedentary lifestyle

4. Anger and depression

5. Negative attitude

THINGS TO DO THAT WILL CORRECT THE PROBLEM

1. Eat correctly

2. Don't smoke

3. Exercise

4. Put joy and laughter into your life

5. Meditate

SUGGESTED DAILY ACTION PLAN

Supplements

1. Vitamin E   100-200 IU (mixed tocopherol)

2. Vitamin C   500 mg

3. Folic Acid   400 mcg

4. Calcium   1000 mg/day

5. Magnesium   500 mg

6. Fish Oil Capsules (if you do not eat fish)

Foods

1. Dark Leafy Vegetables

2. Fatty Fish (3-5 times/week)

3. Soy Products

4. Beans and Grains

5. Berries

6. Nuts (almonds, walnuts, pecans)

7. Fresh garlic (1 clove)

8. Green Tea (1-2 cups)

9. Red Wine (4-5 ounces)

10. Cocoa (1 cup)

11. Olive or Canola Oil

12. Eliminate Saturated and Trans Fats

Exercise and Meditation

At least 30 mins/day

Aspirin

81 mg Enteric coated after meal

10 STEPS FOR COPING

1. Find time daily to meditate.

2. Don't feel like you have to do *everything*.

3. Accept that you have limitations.

4. Develop a support network.

5. Smile and laugh more.

6. Show kindness, pick up liter, open doors for others.

7. Become more spiritual.

8. Get more exercise.

9. Avoid negative people.

10. Maintain a positive attitude.

RISK FACTOR IDENTIFICATION

TAKE THIS WITH YOU
TO YOUR NEXT DOCTOR'S APPOINTMENT

Traditional Risk Factors to be Checked

1. Blood Pressure

2. Cholesterol

3. HDL, LDL, Triglicerides

4. HDL/Cholesterol Ratio

5. Blood Sugar (test for diabetes)

6. BMI and Abdominal Girth

New Risk Factor Tests

1. C-Reactive Protein (CRP)

2. Homocysteine

3. Discuss role of anger, hostility, and depression

Index

<u>NOTES</u>

NOTES

NOTES

9 781425 956493